How to Overcome Depression

How to Overcome Depression

Matilda Nordtvedt

MOODY PRESS
CHICAGO

Original title: *Defeating Despair and Depression*

Library of Congress Cataloging-in-Publication Data

Nordtvedt, Matilda.
    How to overcome depression.
    Rev. ed. of: Defeating despair & depression. 1975.
Personal narratives.   3. Christian life—1960—
I. Nordtvedt, Matilda. Defeating despair & depression.
II. Title.
BR1725.N54A33   1986   248.8′6   85-28401
ISBN 0-8024-1700-0 (pbk.)

    1 2 3 4 5 6 7 Printing/DB/Year 88 87 86
    Printed in the United States of America.

To my husband, who understood and helped me
through my tunnel

CONTENTS

CHAPTER | PAGE

1. My Dark Tunnel — 9
2. My Nervous Breakdown — 12
3. The Psychiatric Ward — 15
4. A Christian in a Tunnel? — 22
5. I Started My Day with Worry — 28
6. As a Man Thinketh — 34
7. It Was of God — 41
8. I Began to Give Thanks — 48
9. The Grumble Rumble — 56
10. Everything Is Against Me — 61
11. Calling Card of the Devil — 64
12. What About Diet? — 69
13. Too Busy or Too Lazy? — 75
14. Everybody Needs a Project — 78
15. There Is Treasure in Trouble — 84
16. A New Chapter in Life's Book — 91
17. God Loves Me — 94
18. Guard Your Link with God — 99
19. In Acceptance Lieth Peace — 102
20. Only True Basis for Happiness — 111
21. Are You So Foolish? — 115
22. It Must Be a Daily Victory — 119
23. A Tunnel or a Pit? — 123
24. Do I Want Deliverance? — 127
25. If Your Loved One Is in a Tunnel — 131
26. Rejoice! — 134

Acknowledgments

Truth is not new, but it becomes new to a person in times of specific need. I am sure that many of the truths brought out in this book came to me through my husband—who is also my pastor—as I sat under his preaching through the years, as well as from other sermons I have heard and books I have read. But head knowledge is different from knowledge experienced. Making these truths experientially mine required a dark tunnel. I am thankful for those who instructed me and also for the tunnel, where I was forced to put those teachings into practice. Most of all, I thank God, who patiently taught a slow learner throughout the years and continues to do so.

1

My Dark Tunnel

Mornings had always been my favorite time of the day. Now I dreaded them. Even the sun shining brightly into our bedroom window and the early morning song of the birds did nothing to bolster my spirits. The thought of facing the stark reality of another day overwhelmed me. How could I endure another fifteen or sixteen hours of meaningless monotony?

I had been a happy person, full of zest for living. Even housework had been challenging and satisfying. But not now. My everyday duties loomed before me like an insurmountable mountain, one I must climb wearily before night fell.

When invited to a friend's home for a meal, I anticipated pleasure such as I had known before when visiting friends. Instead, I was bored and could not wait to leave. Dutifully I attended bridal and baby showers and weddings at our church, but I did not enjoy them. They all seemed so useless and without meaning.

Funerals were even more difficult, especially that of a young man killed in a mill accident. My heart ached with the parents. Everything was heartbreaking. Why did there have to be such tragedy? Would I experience it in my life? I was afraid.

I could not stand to watch the news on television or read the newspaper. It was all too sad: starving orphans, young people on drugs, friends contemplating divorce. I worried: about myself; would I ever be normal and happy again? About the church work; would the people continue to want us? About my children; if sudden death overtook them, would they be ready to meet God?

Nothing pleased me anymore. Nothing seemed worthwhile. Occasionally I had a good day when life seemed a little brighter, but the bright spots were overshadowed by the fear they would not last. They didn't. The darkness returned with alarming consistency.

I kept occupied during the days with work around the house, but the long summer evenings seemed endless. I looked forward eagerly to going to bed, to escape from my depression in pill-induced oblivion. But those hours between dinner and bedtime! Often my husband was busy with meetings or other pastoral duties, so I spent many evenings alone. I did a great deal of walking, up one street and down the other. I looked at the houses and wondered about the people who lived in them. Were they happy? How could they be? I wasn't, even though I had a personal relationship with God, a kind husband, a loving family, and a lovely home. Everything was sad and dark, and frightening. No wonder people jumped off bridges or shot themselves. There wasn't much to live for anyway.

Oh, I would not take my own life. But secretly I longed to die and go to heaven. Then I would not be depressed. I would be happy.

This was my dark tunnel.

2

My Nervous Breakdown

L. Gilbert Little, the Christian medical doctor who wrote *Nervous Christians*, states that the term *nervous breakdown* is really a misnomer. The nerves do not break down, as the term implies. Perhaps *nervous exhaustion* would be more exact.

From the time of my childhood I feared mental illness. Maybe it was because a close friend of our family went berserk when, at fifty years of age, she gave birth to her first child. Shortly after the baby was born, our friend had to be admitted to a mental institution. Mrs. B. came home after several months, but she was never able to stay long. She had to go back periodically. She did not seem crazy, just unusually quiet and unlike her old, jolly self. I decided, when I observed her, that mental illness was the worst of all maladies.

After finishing Bible school I married a seminary student and became a housewife and mother. During times of stress through the years I sometimes worried about cracking up. What if *I* ended up in a mental institution? I could think of nothing more terrifying. God comforted me with the words from

Psalm 139:10, taken out of context perhaps but just the reassurance I needed: "Even there your hand will guide me, your right hand will hold me fast."

Twice while my husband and I served as missionaries in Japan, we were forced to come home early because of my health. The doctor called it nervous exhaustion. After a rest I was able to carry on quite normally again, although I had to be careful not to overdo. At the age of forty-two in a new parish in Grand Forks, North Dakota, I felt myself headed for another breakdown. I seemed compelled to take on more than I could handle. Why, I asked myself, did I attempt to do more than ever just when I was the most tired?

I remember my panicky feeling when the church's college students were to come over for a supper one Sunday evening. I fixed the food, but I just could not face the rest of it. A kind friend came to my rescue, took the food, and held the supper at her home. I was both relieved and ashamed. But I did not learn. Not long afterward, I invited a large group of people again—and again had to be rescued. It left me feeling like a first-class failure.

I began to cry over nothing, sometimes for hours at a time. Why did everything seem so difficult, almost impossible? *I can't give in,* I told myself. *I have to keep trying, keep convincing myself and others that I'm all right. I've got to quit being a baby, got to get hold of myself. It's all in my mind. I don't have to be this way.*

One Sunday morning I decided it was time to snap out of it. I would go to church and sing in the choir as usual. But just before the choir took its place I was seized by an awful fear. "I can't go up there," I said to the woman next to me. She said nothing, just reached out and squeezed my hand. I will never forget that little gesture of kindness. Even though I was acting strangely, she did not despise me. That helped, but the tears began to spill over. I fled from the church. It was an unexplainable anguish. If only I could understand myself!

The next morning I was so desperate for help that I asked my husband to call the doctor, who had been treating me with tranquilizers for several months. Now he recommended that I go to the psychiatric ward of the local hospital. Like Job, that which I greatly feared had come upon me.

This chapter is taken from the article "My Nervous Breakdown," in the July 1971 issue of *Eternity*, pp. 12-13, 39. Reprinted by permission of *Eternity* Magazine, copyright 1971, Evangelical Ministries, Inc., 1716 Spruce Street, Philadelphia, Pa. 19103.

3
The Psychiatric Ward

I will never forget the strange feeling that passed over me when I registered at the hospital. I signed myself in. My husband accompanied me to the fifth-floor psychiatric ward. Even though a notice warned visitors to stop in the foyer, he went with me to my room.

My roommate, Abigail,* was in her early sixties, with dyed-black hair, a large nose, and bright red lipstick. At first glance she reminded me of a witch. I did not feel very reassured as I kissed my husband good-bye and watched him walk down the corridor.

All the nurses wore street clothes. The absence of uniforms was designed to create a homelike atmosphere for the patients. As a brisk, little nurse helped me unpack, she asked me to give her any sharp or glass objects in my purse or suitcase. I surrendered my nail scissors and file, and even my deodorant, feeling a little indignant all the while. Did they think I intended to gouge out my eyes or slash my wrists?

*Names in this chapter have been changed.

The nurse showed me around the ward. First she led me to the day-room, a large lounge where I would spend my days with the other patients. There were games, magazines, newspapers, and TV for our enjoyment. She then showed me the kitchen. I was free to help myself anytime to the fruit juices and ice cream in the refrigerator and even to stir up a cake if I felt like baking.

I didn't. I felt like crying. As soon as possible I made my way back to my room and lay down. But how could I cry here? The nurse insisted I leave the door open at all times, except when I was dressing.

We ate in the day-room. I felt shy at dinner that night. Curious, too. Why were these people here? They all looked normal enough. There were some elderly people, some fortyish like myself, some in their twenties and thirties, and even several teenagers. What would teenagers be doing in a place like this?

I got acquainted with my roommate after dinner. She kept telling me she was so nervous she did not know what to do. She colored nearly every sentence with profanity.

The second day I shared a little booklet with Abigail that showed her the way of salvation. She broke down and cried and prayed the sinner's prayer. I do not think she really came to faith in Christ, but she did start reading *Good News for Modern Man,* a modern version of the New Testament that someone had left in the room. Whenever I read my Bible, Abigail would get her New Testament. When something struck her, she would read it out loud. "Ain't that cute!" she would exclaim about the words of Jesus.

I made friends with Sheila, too, a high school

sophomore who claimed she had lost her faith and was afraid of God's judgment. I talked to her a long time, explaining the way back to God.

After these opportunities to witness, I decided the psychiatric ward was not so bad after all. I was there for a reason. "Even there your hand will guide me." It was exciting, especially several days later when Sheila came to me to say she believed in God again.

"I'm sure lucky that you came here," she said. "God sent you here for me."

I mounted cloud nine.

Then Connie came, a tiny, young housewife and mother with sad eyes. She was unsure of herself and eager to please. She welcomed my friendship and was hungry to hear about the Lord. I showed her the way of salvation from the Bible. With tears streaming down her face, she prayed to receive Christ.

Abigail was still taking God's name in vain in spite of my protests, so I feared she was still in her darkness. But Sheila and Connie showed signs of genuine conversion. They sought me out whenever they had an opportunity. Sheila even came to talk and ask questions before I was out of bed in the morning. Finally it got to me. I was not strong enough to cope with these two spiritual babies. It was like giving birth to twins and not being able to take care of them.

Meanwhile the nurses had kept an eye on us and reported to the psychiatrist. The result was that Sheila was relieved of her Bible and told to stop seeing me; I was told to stop worrying about everybody else and start loving myself a little. (My husband insists I was giving the psychiatrist too much competition!)

The psychiatrist gave me large doses of drugs. When this did not seem to solve the problem, he recommended gas shock treatments (similar to electric).

Shock treatments for *me?* A few days before, Abigail had taken her first one. She was so afraid she cried piteously the night before.

"It's nothing, Abigail," I assured her. "They'll put you out, so you won't know what's happening. It's nothing to be afraid of."

But now I was not so sure. I woke up that morning to find a sign on the head of my bed: "Nothing by mouth." Not even a drink of water! I have to admit that, like Abigail, I was scared. Then my special verse came to mind and gave me courage: "even *there* your hand will guide me, your right hand will hold me fast" (Psalm 139:10, italics mine). I was repeating the verse quietly to myself when the orderly wheeled me into the treatment room, and the doctor stuck a needle in my arm to put me to sleep.

When I woke up several hours later in my own bed, I had a stiff neck and felt a little nauseated but was all right otherwise. *He* was still with me as He had promised.

The shock treatments, designed to take the patient out of the world of unreality and make it possible for him to accept actualities, often cause temporary confusion and loss of memory. Although not a cure in itself, the treatment puts the patient in a favorable condition for cure. Drugs do essentially the same thing, sometimes more effectively. I had both treatments.

Nurses and aides of the psychiatric ward tried to create a cheerful atmosphere for us. They persuaded Martha, a woman in her late sixties, to make cinnamon rolls for us. We spent several hours a day in the crafts room making things. I laced a small leather purse in the shape of a moccasin for my oldest son's girl friend, laboriously plaited a leather belt for my husband, and decoupaged pictures for my sons.

We were all assigned to clean-up chores. When it was my turn to clean the day-room, I started to give it a thorough going over. Magazines had not been straightened for a long time, and the shelves for games were a mess! But the aide stopped me. "That's good enough," she said when I finished dusting. I got the feeling they were just trying to keep us busy and did not want us to get involved in any exacting work. I enjoyed the exercise periods and the supervised walks around the hospital grounds. I looked forward eagerly to telephone time, when I could talk with my family, and visiting days when they could come to see me.

But the depressing things heavily outweighed the bright moments. Attractive, blond, seventeen-year-old Lori was crying one day because she was being sent to the state institution. Sally, a pretty twenty-four-year-old woman was there because she could not cope with caring for her baby. Every time she tried to feed him she saw double, and "two babies" were just too much! Celia, sophisticated and sad, asked, "Have you ever felt as if you didn't love your husband and kids?" Martha was simply unbearably depressed. Connie had marital problems. Sheila was confused. There was a great scurrying around one night when Bill, a thirty-year-old alcoholic, slashed his wrists. We never knew where he got the razor or whatever he used.

Abigail smoked heavily, but it was against rules to smoke in the rooms. She hated to go to the day-room or kitchen in the middle of the night to smoke, so she would hide matches in her pocket and sneak a smoke in our bathroom. One night when the nurses made their periodic check, they smelled the smoke.

"Abigail, have you got matches?" they asked. "Have you been smoking in the bathroom?"

Abigail could lie without flickering an eyelash. "Nope, not me!" she declared stoutly.

I grinned to myself under the covers, feeling like a teenager rebelling against the establishment. I was not about to tell on Abigail.

I had gone home on a number of occasions during my stay in the hospital, and my family had come to see me often. It was a happy day when, after being hospitalized for four weeks, I learned that I could go home for good.

The doctor recommended a trip. It was time for my husband's vacation, so this worked out fine. With two of our three teenaged sons, we drove to Washington State and then to California. The scenery was beautiful. There were bright spots—like picnics beside the road, Disneyland, and seeing loved ones—but for the most part I was miserable. I could not understand why it was not fun to visit relatives and friends anymore. I was tense, nervous, and extremely depressed. I begged my husband to cut our vacation short and take me home, sure that when I got home I would be my old, happy self again.

But I was not. I was depressed, in a dark tunnel from which I could not escape, no matter how much I cried and prayed. This continued, with only occasional rays of light, for over six months.

The next chapters tell how God brought me out of the tunnel and about the wonderful lessons He taught me enroute.

Portions of this chapter are taken from the article "My Nervous Breakdown," in the July 1971 issue of *Eternity*, pages 12-13, 39. Reprinted by permission of *Eternity* Magazine, copyright 1971, Evangelical Ministries, Inc., 1716 Spruce Street, Philadelphia, Pa. 19103.

4

A Christian in a Tunnel?

I used to shake my head at the thought of Christians suffering from nervous exhaustion and emotional illness. Certainly a "spiritual" Christian would not get himself into a fix like that!

It is true that many Christians bring on their own emotional troubles by carnal living, ambition, selfishness, or lack of communion with God. Saul, the first king of Israel, is a good example. My heart aches when I read his tragic story, realizing that it is the story of thousands in our world today. Saul started out well: humble, brave, obedient to God; but he ended in despair, forsaken by God, a suicide. What happened to bring him to such an end?

The road down is always gradual. Who knows Saul's first step away from God? Was it the entertainment of some secret sin in the depths of his heart? Was it neglect in spending time with God? The Bible does not tell us. The first hint that he was slipping is found in 1 Samuel 13, a time of crisis. Saul faced a great enemy army, and his soldiers were deserting him. Samuel was to offer a burnt offering and peace offering and to pray for Israel, but he did not come at the appointed time. Saul became impatient. There was danger in delay. Fear and unbelief caused him to intrude into the priest's office and offer the burnt offering himself.

Moments later Samuel came and rebuked him severely. We have no record that Saul repented of this sin. We only see him as he strayed further and further away from God. A desire for popularity with his people and prestige led him to disobey God in the matter of destroying the Amalekites. When Samuel rebuked him for this sin, his only concern seemed to be to retain his good image before the people. He had taken himself and his affairs out of the hands of God and was trying to manage them himself. The result was severe mental depression. We read in 1 Samuel 16:14 (TLB*), "But the Spirit of the Lord had left Saul, and instead, the Lord had sent a tormenting spirit that filled him with depression and fear."

Although it is true that some cases of mental depression are the result of disobedience, as in Saul's case, this is not always the case. Others are living close to God when they become emotionally ill. What is the explanation for this? As I look back at my own experience, I realize that each time before a plunge into the dark, I had been enjoying a spiritual "high." God was very near and precious to me and His work exciting. Why, then, the plunge?

It could have been pride, which we know is always followed by a fall. Maybe I was taking my eyes off the Lord and getting too excited about what

The Living Bible.

He was doing and my small part in it (see chapter 20).

On the other hand, Satan is after the Christian who lives close to God and is being used by Him. He does not need to bother about the carnal one who does little to harm his kingdom. Certainly he is eager to stop the earnest Christian by his oppression and evil suggestions.

Have you ever noticed how often depression and darkness come on the heels of a great spiritual victory? Shortly before a bout of nervous exhaustion in Japan, I had received such wonderful news that I walked on clouds for several days. Mrs. Yamada, a beautiful, cultured, middle-aged woman who had been attending our ladies' meetings, confessed her faith in Christ. Middle-aged or older people are hard to win to Christ in any culture, but especially in Japan, where religious and family ties are tightly interwoven. Mrs. Yamada's conversion was truly a miracle of God, as well as the key to the hearts of the other women of the group. We were elated.

Now as I look back, does it not seem strange that just after this moment of great triumph in the work of God I should suffer a nervous collapse and have to go away for a long rest? Elijah experienced a tremendous victory on Mount Carmel when he called down fire from heaven and put to shame the prophets of Baal. When he prayed for rain after three years of drought, his prayer was gloriously answered. But what do we see him doing after all this victory? He ran from Jezebel, sat under a juniper tree, and requested that he die.

Weariness no doubt accounted for some of Elijah's depression. The Lord must have realized this, because He gave him sleep and food saying, "The journey is too much for you" (1 Kings 19:7b). Yes, victory can be exhausting. We can become emotionally drained also from much joy. Satan is quick to take advantage of any weakness he detects. We are not expecting him, and down we go.

I have a friend who has also experienced "the tunnel" and often has periods of depression. She says that during these times she has doubts even about her salvation. This is suffering, indeed, but I believe it is unnecessary suffering. As Jesus said in the parable of the tares and wheat, "An enemy did this" (Matthew 13:28).

Satan is delighted when we listen to him instead of to God. That is what Eve did, remember? When you doubt your salvation after you have sincerely received Christ as your Savior, you are taking Satan's word instead of God's. He knows your vulnerability at this point and makes the most of it in tormenting you with doubts. Have I really been forgiven? Am I a Christian? If I am, why do I feel this way?

Many earnest Christians suffer from guilt feelings, even after they have confessed all known sin to God. There is an uneasy feeling within that all is not well. The Holy Spirit convicts us of specific sins so we can repent of them and receive forgiveness from God. That nagging uneasiness is not from Him. It may be a part of our psychological makeup, or it may be the devil tormenting us.

Francis Schaeffer, in his book *True Spirituality*, put it this way: "We may know, as the value of Christ's death is infinite, so all the true guilt in us is covered, and the guilty feelings that remain are not true guilt, but a part of these awful miseries of fallen man: out of the historic fall, out of the life of the race, and out of my own personal past."[1]

Recognizing that these feelings are not from God helps us to disregard them and rejoice instead that "therefore, there is now no condemnation for those who are in Christ Jesus" (Romans 8:1).

Do not let Satan have the last word. Turn to God's Word, and see what God says. If He says it, believe it, regardless of feelings. Confess your doubts to Him as the sin they are. Ask Him for power to resist your enemy. In the all-powerful name of Jesus tell Satan to take his evil suggestions and be gone! Do as Jesus did when Satan tempted Him; say, "It is written" (Luke 4:1-12). In the face of God's Word Satan will have to run. Remember that Satan, who puts doubts into our minds as well as other troublesome thoughts that lead to depression, is a defeated foe. Through Christ we can claim victory over his oppression.

Satan is not always the author of our darkness, however. Sometimes God sends darkness into the life of His child to teach him something he could not learn in the light. Isaiah says, "Who among you fears the Lord and obeys the word of his servant? Let him who walks in the dark, who has no light, trust in the name of the Lord and rely on his God" (Isaiah 50:10). From this passage we may conclude that it is possible for an obedient Christian also to experience periods of darkness.

T. S. Rendall of Prairie Bible Institute, in his booklet *The Discipline of Darkness,* gives helpful directions

1. Francis Schaeffer, *True Spirituality* (Wheaton, Ill.: Tyndale, 1971), p. 133.

to the obedient Christian who finds himself in the dark. "In the light of God's Word, you need first to identify the darkness as coming from God; second, you must interpret its purpose; and finally you must seek to derive personal blessing from the discipline."[2] In other words, ask yourself, "What is God trying to teach me through this experience?"

As we mature as Christians, we learn to walk by faith apart from feelings and outward manifestations of God's love. How pleased God must be when we trust Him implicitly, even in the dark; and remember, the darkness will not last forever. After we have learned the important lessons God has for us, He will "lighten our darkness," even as He did for the psalmist.

As Paul said, "All things are yours" (1 Corinthians 3:21). Yes, even the night!

5

I Started My Day with Worry

Our bedroom faces north and east, so we get the morning sun. During the days of my depression I usually woke up very early, after the effects of my strong tranquilizer had worn off. Sunshine and bird songs did nothing to cheer me. My first thought was an anxious one, as if someone seized my mind and took possession of it as soon as I became conscious. Now I know it was Satan trying to tyrannize me.

My worries varied with the morning. Sometimes they were about my children, the awful things that might happen to them. Sometimes I worried about my husband dying and leaving me. Sometimes I was seized with the fear of returning to the psychiatric ward and this time really losing all control of myself.

Sometimes my worries were over silly little things; but how big they became as I lay in bed and let my imagination run wild. How I dreaded the mental torture of those early morning hours!

I also worried throughout the day. When my oldest son left for a job in another part of the state, I worried about him so much I became physically ill.

When someone lent me the book *How to Win over Worry,* by John Haggai, I devoured it as a starving man devours food. The first thing that hit me as I read the book was that worry is a sin. God commands us not to worry; and if we do, we sin against Him. I read how many physical diseases are caused by worry; ulcers, colitis, heart trouble, high blood pressure, arthritis, and even colds. A noted physician states that 75 percent of the people who go to doctors could cure themselves if they got rid of their worries and fears.

John Haggai said, "Worry is an intrusion into God's providence. You are making yourself the father of the household instead of the child."[1]

I had learned to trust God for many things during my years as a Christian. We had experienced rather lean years financially while in Japan and in various pastorates afterwards, but I seldom worried about finances. It was exciting to see God provide. But I had not learned to trust Him for the salvation of my loved ones, especially my children.

The story of Monica, Augustine's mother, rebuked my lack of faith. Monica worried about her son, Augustine. He went from one excess to another, dabbling in sinful pleasures, aesthetic delights, and false philosophies. His latest whim was to go to Rome. How Monica prayed that he would not leave her influence and go to the wicked city. One night Monica awoke with a strange feeling that all was not well. Going to her son's room, she found it empty. She ran out into the night, but reached the dock

1. John E. Haggai, *How to Win over Worry* (Grand Rapids: Zondervan, 1959), p. 142.

too late to stop her son. The ship had set sail for Rome.

Monica was heartbroken, but she need not have been. God answered her prayer *His* way. In Rome her son heard of an opening in Milan for a professor of rhetoric, and he obtained the position. There he met the godly bishop whose influence caused him to seek God earnestly and become a Christian, one that God has mightily used through the years.

One mother with wayward children told me, "If I couldn't commit my children to God and trust Him to save them, I'd lose my mind." She had learned the secret of trusting God, and so experienced peace instead of worry.

Another friend (I'll call her Helen) found herself waking up at night, besieged by worry. As she worried about family problems she could not go back to sleep. Sometimes she got up and prowled the house. The next day she was completely exhausted and unable to do her work. Then a new worry presented itself—what would happen to her if she kept having these sleepless nights? She could already feel herself getting sick.

Just at this time Helen was asked to lead a group of women in a neighborhood Bible study. The subject was prayer. Almost overwhelmed by her own problems, she wondered how she could take on this extra activity. But she did, albeit reluctantly. The emphasis of the course was on believing God. *Are you just praying words, or do you really believe God hears you and that He will answer as He promised? Is He able to work out your problems for you? How big is God, anyway? What about His promises? Can't you depend on them?*

Nobody got as much out of the Bible study as Helen did. She learned to take God at His word, and that took care of the worry. As she realized anew that she could turn her family and her cares over to a loving, powerful, heavenly Father, she was able to sleep through the night again. Helen's problems are not all solved yet, but she is trusting God to solve them. She has exchanged her worry for trust and peace.

David worried, too. Sometimes he even imagined that God had forsaken him. In Psalm 77:7 he asks, "Will the Lord reject us forever? Will he never show his favor again? Has his unfailing love vanished forever? Has his promise failed for all time? Has God forgotten to be merciful? Has he in anger with-held his compassion?" Foolish questions, aren't they?

David found the answer as he *remembered* what God had done for him in the past. He said, "I will remember." As he remembered how God had come to his rescue so many times before, he knew his fears and doubts were groundless. Remembering what God had done for him in the past gave him courage and comfort for the present and future.

Remembering will help us, too. Has not God answered prayers before? Has He not worked out things that seemed impossible? Has He changed, that we should doubt and worry?

John Wesley said: "I feel and grieve, but by the grace of God I fret at nothing."[2] This great preacher attributed his good health partly to having so little sorrow and anxious care.

---

2. John Wesley, *The Journal of John Wesley* (Chicago: Moody, n.d.), p. 406.

It has taken me a long time to learn to trust, to cast my cares on the Lord: my family, my friends, my relatives, the work of the Lord, the world situation, myself. After my long practice of worrying it seemed almost indecent to stop. It was almost as though I were being selfish, not to be doing "my bit." Over and over again I had to remind myself that worrying did not help. It was sin, because it made God a liar and made me ill. God says through the psalmist, "Do not fret—it only leads to evil" (Psalm 37:8). Jesus said, "Who of you by worrying can add a single hour to his life? Since you cannot do this very thing, why do you worry about the rest?" (Luke 12:25-26). God said through Paul, "Do not be anxious about anything, but in everything, by prayer and petition, with thanksgiving, present your requests to God" (Philippians 4:6).

Thank Him for the answers? Even before they come? Isn't that audacity? No, it is faith. Jesus said, "According to your faith will it be done to you" (Matthew 9:29); "It will be done just as you believed it would" (Matthew 8:13); "Therefore I tell you, whatever you ask for in prayer, believe that you have received it, and it will be yours" (Mark 11:24).

Larry Christenson, in his book *The Christian Family*, urges Christians to use creative imagination when they pray. "Visualize that person or that situation the way it's going to be when God enters in," he says. "See the answer instead of the problem."[3]

I began to understand that I should thank God in advance for what He was doing for my loved ones

3. Larry Christenson, *The Christian Family* (Minneapolis: Bethany, 1970), pp. 177, 188.

and for what He was going to do. I stopped begging and started thanking. I began to learn to take my burdens to the Lord and leave them there.

I discovered that worry thoughts would crowd in again and again and overwhelm me unless I continually replaced them with trust thoughts. Where did I get the trust thoughts? From God's Word. That is another reason that Bible reading and memorization have became so important to me. God's promises are my bulwark against Satan's attacks on my mind. They are my answer to his invitation to worry.

To discover this was another step toward the light.

6

As a Man Thinketh

Negative thinking is first cousin to depression. They work together to drag a person down. During my "tunnel days" my thinking was almost always negative, like Jacob from the Old Testament.

Jacob was God's man. He valued what God valued—the birthright and the blessing—even if he did so in the wrong way. God changed Jacob's name to *Israel*, meaning *prince of God*, because of his determination to receive God's best. Jacob was a great man in many respects, but I wonder how much greater he could have been if he had maintained a positive attitude instead of a negative one throughout his life.

Although God blessed Jacob with a large family and many riches, we hear him complaining instead of thanking God. To his father-in-law he grumbled, "This was my situation: The heat consumed me in the daytime and the cold at night, and sleep fled from my eyes" (Genesis 31:40). No mention of the riches God had given him.

When Jacob's sons brought him Joseph's blood-stained coat, Jacob refused to be comforted; he evidently preferred to wallow in self-pity: "in mourning will I go down to the grave to my son" (Genesis 37:35). Later, when his sons went to Egypt to buy grain and came back telling him the ruler of the land had kept Simeon in jail and demanded they bring Benjamin with them when they came again, Jacob wailed, "Everything is against me!" (Genesis 42:36).

When Jacob had been reunited with Joseph in Egypt, he was presented to Pharaoh. What did he say to the monarch of Egypt? "The years of my pilgrimage are a hundred and thirty. My years have been few and difficult, and they do not equal the years of the pilgrimage of my fathers" (Genesis 47:9). In spite of his recent reunion with Joseph he was still gloomy, negative, not praising God.

Contrast Joseph to his father. He had many more things against him than did Jacob: the jealousy and hatred of his brothers; separation from his home under cruel circumstances; slavery in Egypt; false accusation by Potiphar's wife; imprisonment; disappointment when he was forgotten by one he had befriended.

The Bible is an extremely honest Book. If Joseph had complained, I believe it would have been recorded. But there is no mention made of any complaining or of feeling sorry for himself. Rather, Joseph trusted God and waited for Him to make his dreams reality.

Joseph made the best of his situation, both at Potiphar's house and in jail. At both places he was given positions of responsibility, something that could not have happened if Joseph had been bitter and sulky.

Out of prison at last, and ruler of Egypt! Joseph

named his two sons Manasseh, which means "forgetting" (the bitter things that had happened to him) and Ephraim, meaning "fruitful," because God had caused him to be fruitful in the land of his affliction. Catch the positive note here? There was no sulking, no self-pity. He put the bitterness of the past from his mind and rejoiced in the blessings of the present.

Joseph harbored no resentment against his brothers but saw God's hand working even through their wickedness. He said to them, when he revealed who he was: "Do not be distressed and do not be angry with yourselves for selling me here, because it was to save lives that God sent me ahead of you. . . . So then, it was not you who sent me here, but God" (Genesis 45:5, 8). Later he reassured them by saying, "Don't be afraid . . . You intended to harm me, but God intended it for good" (Genesis 50:19-20).

Paul was another positive thinker. If you want a lift, read the epistle to the Philippians. Paul, though in prison, found many things to be glad about: "What has happened to me has really served to advance the gospel" (Philippians 1:12). Even after speaking about his enemies, who were trying to add to his suffering in prison, he said triumphantly, "I rejoice. Yes, and I will continue to rejoice, for I know that through your prayers and the help given by the Spirit of Jesus Christ, what has happened to me will turn out for my deliverance" (Philippians 1:18-19). Later he urged, "Whatever happens, dear friends, be glad in the Lord. . . . Always be full of joy in the Lord. . . . Think about all you can praise God for and be glad about. . . . Fix your thoughts on what is true and good and right. Think about things that are pure and lovely, and dwell on the fine, good things in others" (Philippians 4:8, TLB).

Dwell on the fine, good things in others? That goes for a husband or wife as well as other people. Do we not more often dwell on the bad points in our mates and friends?

A woman with a problem came to visit us recently: she was not getting along well with her husband. He was stubborn, dictatorial, and did not show her the affection she craved. As she told us about her husband's faults she would interject such things as: "I'll have to admit he is a good provider; he's a good father to the children; he doesn't criticize me; I know he loves me even if he doesn't always show it." By the end of the counseling session, to her surprise this woman had found more good points than bad ones in her husband. As she thought about the good things, the bad ones that had seemed so big and aggravating grew smaller and insignificant. When she left she realized she had a pretty good husband after all. Although he might never change some of his characteristics that aggravated her, she could put up with them if she concentrated on his good points and praised God for them.

There is another thing we should keep in mind when we find it hard to get along with someone. God has given us just the right parents, mates, children, and associates to develop the Christian graces in our lives. We should praise God for patience and the other virtues that are becoming a part of our characters through their maddening habits and inconsistencies. It is all for our good! Think of it positively, and thank God.

My friend Sue* became a Christian about two years ago. Her husband refuses to attend church with her. She spends many evenings alone with her four small children while he is out drinking with his friends. But she rarely indulges in self-pity. She makes the best of her situation and develops interests and friendships to keep her busy. She also looks for the good points in her husband and dwells on those instead of on the bad ones. As she tries hard to be a good wife, she prays in faith that he will one day come to Christ. Her positive attitude is like a breath of fresh air. And it is getting results; her husband is beginning to change in his attitudes.

What is positive thinking but faith—faith that God will do what He has promised, make everything work together for the good of the child of God? Life is different when we make ourselves look at the bright side and thank God instead of wallowing in gloom and unbelief. "The mind of sinful man is death, but the mind controlled by the Spirit is life and peace" (Romans 8:6). Self pity is the mind of sinful man; so are grumbling, complaining, discontent, worry, fear, and unbelief. I have experienced the "living death" of the mind of sinful man, and you probably have too. Oh, the joy of spiritual-mindedness, of faith and trust in the love and wisdom of God! This is the path to life and peace.

God told the Israelites through Moses that He was giving them a choice of life or death: life if they went His way, death if they went their own. He said to them, "Now choose life, so that you and your children may live" (Deuteronomy 30:19).

*Name has been changed.

"The spiritual battle, the loss of victory, is always in the thought-world," says Francis Schaeffer in *True Spirituality*.[1] Our minds are so constructed that we can concentrate on only one thing at a time. When plagued by negative, destructive thoughts, I have found it is possible to replace them with positive, uplifting ones. It is not always easy, especially for those who have established a pattern of pessimism, but it is possible.

One great antidote for gloomy thoughts is good old-fashioned work: scrub a floor, clean out a closet, make a company dinner, rake the yard. Such tasks require enough concentration to keep us from dwelling on depressing things.

Negative thoughts often come swarming into the mind at night. A friend of mine, who lives alone, gets up and bakes cookies at 2:00 A.M. rather than lie awake and think gloomy thoughts. Those of us with families probably cannot do this, but there are other ways to replace negative thoughts with positive ones. The very best way I know is to meditate on Scripture. I suggested memorizing Scripture to a discouraged friend, and she immediately answered, "I'm too old to memorize any more." I challenge that statement. My eighty-two-year-old relative recently memorized the entire fifth chapter of Matthew, all forty-eight verses, almost word perfect! No doubt it is harder to memorize now than when we were younger, but I cannot believe it is impossible. The harder the better, really.

I have found so many truths in the first chapter of

1. Schaeffer, *True Spirituality* (Wheaton, Ill.: Tyndale, 1971), p. 222.

Philippians since I started to memorize it. I have to go over it again and again before it sticks in my memory, and each time I get a new blessing. It becomes a part of me. Even if I do not retain it all, I have benefited immeasurably from having tried. In the night, when I cannot sleep and Satan tries to oppress me with his suggestions, snatches of Scripture come to mind to help drive him away. Bill Gothard, instructor of the Institute in Basic Youth Conflicts, stated that the devil would rather have a Christian sleep than meditate on Scripture. So if we start meditating, he will stop trying to keep us awake with troublesome thoughts.

Prayer is a good antidote for unwelcome thoughts, too, but praise is even better. We need a whole chapter to discuss that important subject, but first, let me share with you a life-changing discovery.

7

It Was of God

"If only the ambulance had come right away when I called," the grieving widow said, "my husband might not have died. Or if my doctor had consented to my taking him to Rochester as I suggested!" These "if" thoughts tormented my bereaved neighbor. I hastened to assure her that it was of God that her husband was taken when he was. It was a part of His perfect plan for them. Only when she accepted it as His will would she find peace.

"Is God in Everything?" is the title of a chapter of Hannah Whitall Smith's book *The Christian's Secret of a Happy Life*. Her answer is an unequivocal yes.

During my tunnel experience I came upon this wonderful chapter and began to understand a truth that changed my life. In my depression I had puzzled over many things. My mental anguish was intensified as I heard of the sufferings of others. I could not bear to listen to the news on TV, to see the war-torn villages, the homeless children, the starving people. I could not bear to hear about couples contemplating divorce, children disappointing their parents, elderly people languishing in loneliness.

Nothing made sense until I came across those words, "See God in everything."

In everything? I had always been able to see God in some things: financial difficulties caused me to trust Him more; illness taught me patience; the death of loved ones made me more heavenly minded. I recognized these adversities as blessings in disguise. But *everything*, Lord? The unkindness of Christians? The waywardness of children? What about our friend's son who ran away from home to join a group of hippies? You could not be in that!

Romans 8:28 reads, "And we know that in all things God works for the good of those who love him," but I had paraphrased it to read, "*Some* things work together for good." Maybe I could go even further and agree that *most* things work for my good; but *all* things? Really believing that would revolutionize my life. I would be able to give thanks in everything, as God commands. Did I dare?

If I believed this, I would see my trouble or trial not always as *originating* with God, for He is not the author of evil, but as *permitted* and *used* by Him. Job's sufferings originated with Satan—they were his idea—but God gave him permission to afflict Job; otherwise he could not have done so.

Our God is so wise, so powerful, that He can bring good out of evil. As Moses told the Israelites concerning Balaam's curse upon them, "the Lord your God . . . turned the curse into a blessing for you" (Deuteronomy 23:5). Our God can do that, impossible as it may seem. Yes, He even uses Satan and his temptations as part of His plan to bring His children to spiritual maturity.

Someone might argue that holding this conviction

would tend to lead people into fatalism, accepting everything in life as inevitable, or as some say, "What is to come, will come, and there's nothing I can do about it." Fatalism attributes everything to *fate*. One who sees God in everything looks in faith to an all-wise, all-knowing, loving heavenly Father, who turns even the evil of the world into something good for His child.

At a women's meeting one day a young woman spoke on this subject. She really believed Romans 8:28. She used Joseph from the Old Testament as her example. Was it *good* that Joseph's brothers were jealous? Was it *good* they sold him into slavery? Was it *good* that Potiphar's wife falsely accused Joseph, with the result he was thrown into prison? Of course not. None of these things were good in themselves. They did not come from God. But God, in His great wisdom and love, worked them *together* for Joseph's good. He used these experiences to train Joseph to become the ruler of Egypt and save Israel, as well as many other people of the world, from starvation during years of famine. Joseph's own testimony was: "You intended to harm me, but God intended it for good" (Genesis 50:20).

It is like making biscuits. The ingredients, shortening, flour, salt, and soda, are not very good by themselves. Taste them and see. But when an expert cook mixes them together in the right proportions, puts them in a pan, and bakes them, there is nothing more delicious! God wants to take the distasteful ingredients of our lives and put them together into something beautiful.

The speaker also brought out the verse following Romans 8:28, which we often overlook. What is the reason for God's permitting these things to come into our lives? That we might be "conformed to the likeness of his Son" (Romans 8:29). He is training us for a specific task as He did Joseph, not only for now but also for the life beyond.

I was eager to talk to the speaker after the meeting, because she put into words just what I had begun to learn. As I talked with her I found out that life had not been easy for her. She was suffering from a physical affliction; besides that, one of her small children was emotionally disturbed. But she took it all as part of God's plan for her, letting God work the difficulties of her life *together* for her good. She was growing into the likeness of Christ. It was beautiful!

What about our failures? Shall we blame God for them? Oh, no! Certainly not! We are responsible for our own actions. Much of our suffering we bring upon ourselves through wrong attitudes and decisions. We go our own way instead of God's and fail miserably. Yet we can benefit even from failure if we let God show us where we have erred and learn the lessons He tries to teach us in allowing us to fail.

If we do not take Romans 8:28 for what it says, we may as well toss it out altogether. Hannah Whitall Smith says, "Nearly everything in life comes to us through human instrumentalities, and most of our trials are the result of somebody's failure, or ignorance, or carelessness, or sin. We know God cannot be the author of these things; and yet, unless He is the agent in the matter, how can we say to Him about it, 'Your will be done'? Besides, what good is there trusting our affairs to God, if, after all, man is to be allowed to come in and disarrange them; and how is it possible to live by faith, if human agencies, in which it would be wrong and foolish to trust, are to have a prevailing influence in moulding our lives?"[1]

I started to read through my Bible to see what I could find about God's hand in the affairs of men. The following is a sample of what I found: "This turn of events was from the Lord." "This is my doing." "Surely these things happened to Judah according to the Lord's command." "For the Lord had determined to frustrate the good advice of Ahithophel." "The king's heart is in the hand of the Lord; he directs it like a watercourse wherever he pleases." "The lot is cast into the lap, but its every decision is from the Lord." "Who can speak and have it happen if the Lord has not decreed it?"

God used man's wrath to praise Him in the case of Moses. Pharaoh determined to kill all the male children of Israel. Moses' mother put him in a basket in the river, where Pharaoh's daughter found him. Pharaoh's daughter was moved to adopt him. When she needed a nurse, Moses' own mother was engaged. (She was able to train him in God's way in his early formative years.) Moses was educated in Pharaoh's court and trained to be the leader of his people. What a beautiful plan hidden in the disaster of Pharaoh's cruel edict!

There is a sentence in the book of Esther that thrills me every time I read it: "That night the king could not sleep; so he ordered the book of the chronicles, the record of his reign, to be brought in

---

1. Hannah Whitall Smith, *The Christian's Secret of a Happy Life* (Old Tappan, N.J.: Revell, 1888, 1916, 1968), pp. 143-44.

and read to him" (Esther 6:1). What is so thrilling about that? You know the story. Haman was plotting to destroy the Jews. He had gone so far as to secure the king's permission. The night before Haman planned to hang Mordecai, Queen Esther's uncle and the champion of the Jews, the king could not sleep and asked for the records to be read to him. In the records he came across an item telling how Mordecai had exposed two watchmen who were planning to assassinate the king. Suddenly the king realized that no reward had been given this man to whom he owed his life.

The next morning—before Haman could request that Mordecai be hanged on the gallows he had constructed for him—because the king had discovered Mordecai's good deed the previous night in the records, the king commanded Haman to clothe Mordecai in royal robes and take him through the streets on the king's own horse, honoring him before all. This was the beginning of Haman's downfall and the subsequent rescue of the Jews from death. It all started with a sleepless night. It was of God! If the king had suffered from insomnia the next night, it would have been too late to save Mordecai and his people. But God is never too late. His timing is perfect. Just at the strategic time He intervened, and the king could not sleep!

David said, "He made known his ways to Moses, his deeds to the people of Israel" (Psalm 103:7). Anyone can see God's acts, even the disobedient Israelites, but not everyone can understand His ways. For instance, do we always realize what God is trying to accomplish for eternity through tragedy? Could this be God's confiding in those who fear Him that David wrote about in Psalm 25—seeing God in everything—even disasters? His ways and thoughts are so much higher than ours. And His wisdom! Behind His acts are His ways, His loving, tender ways to bring us closer to Him and make us more like Him. If we could only learn to recognize them!

I became excited when I began to discover this truth: God is in everything. A shaft of sunlight had penetrated my dark tunnel.

But that is only half the secret!

8

I Began to Give Thanks

With the discovery that God is in everything, I realized I must give thanks for everything. In fact God through Paul commands us to do so: "Give thanks in all circumstances, for this is God's will for you in Christ Jesus" (1 Thessalonians 5:18). When gloomy thoughts crowded into my mind the first thing in the morning, I began to thank God for the blessings I formerly took for granted: the sunshine (or snow or rain), the new day, my family, strength to do my work, the use of my mind and other faculties, friends, a home, food, clothing. I thanked Him for the host of spiritual blessings He had given me: a Savior, forgiveness, peace with Him, eternal life, daily guidance, the Bible. There were other things, too, for which I could give thanks if I stopped to consider. In fact, the more I thought about it, the longer my list grew.

Gradually, imperfectly at first, I began to give thanks not only for my obvious blessings but also for the difficult, hard-to-understand aspects of my life. My down moments became more and more infrequent. About a month after I learned that God is in everything and started giving thanks in earnest, I suddenly realized one day that I was out of my tunnel! I was no longer depressed.

I cannot tell you the gratitude and joy that filled my heart when I realized my days of darkness were over; I was out in the sunshine! Life became interesting again and worth living. Boredom vanished. Whereas during my tunnel days I had often wondered how to make the unpleasant hours pass, now I never had enough hours to do all the things I wanted to do. It is hard to believe the difference in my life, it is so great.

I did not learn to give thanks perfectly in a day. I still have not. But I am learning. I keep reminding myself of the following verses from the Bible: "Give thanks in all circumstances, for this is God's will for you in Christ Jesus" (1 Thessalonians 5:18); "always giving thanks to God the Father for everything, in the name of our Lord Jesus Christ" (Ephesians 5:20); "I will extol the Lord at all times; his praise will always be on my lips," or, "I will praise the Lord no matter what happens" (Psalm 34:1, TLB).

I love the psalms of David because they are so full of praise to God. But think of all the troubles David had, pursued by Saul and betrayed by his own son!

Paul was another "praiser." Remember when he and Silas were in the jail at Philippi? At midnight they prayed and sang praises unto God, and God sent an earthquake to free them.

God worked in response to praise in Old Testament times, too. Before King Jehoshaphat went to battle against the hosts of Moab and Ammon, he committed himself and his nation to God. He urged his people to believe God, then appointed singers to

precede his army, singing praises to the Lord. This
was genuine faith! "As they began to sing and praise,
the Lord set ambushes against the men of Ammon
and Moab and Mount Seir who were invading Judah, and they were defeated" (2 Chronicles 20:22).
The Lord gave Judah a great victory as they *praised*.

Let me give you a modern-day example of how
praise changes things. A Christian couple, friends of
ours, had an extremely wayward son who had
broken their hearts by his sinful activities. They
prayed and prayed for their boy, but nothing
seemed to change. Then they started to praise God,
not, obviously, for the sinfulness of their son—but in
faith, praising Him for what He was going to do for
him and also for what He was doing in their lives
through this trial. The son, who had not been home
for a whole year, called his parents just two weeks
after they had begun to praise and came home to
see them. Although the problems are not all solved
at the time of this writing, the parents are thankful
for the evidence of God's working. They continue to
praise and believe God for ultimate victory over
Satan.

A woman, whose heart had been broken by an
unfaithful husband, confided to me that she did not
get peace and victory in her life until she got down
on her knees and thanked God for her heartbreak.
When she finally gave thanks for this dark experience of her life, the terrible hurt was replaced by
peace.

Praise the Lord, Anyway is the appealing title of
one of Frances Gardiner Hunter's helpful books. I
taped this caption over my sink so I can see it every
day. Sometimes I forget to praise, but when I remember, even the grimmest situation becomes bear-

able and the darkest day bright.

When vacation time approached this year I could hardly wait to get going. I could see myself by a beautiful lake, swimming, hiking, reading, and soaking up sunshine. But things did not turn out the way we had planned. The lake was beautiful but too cold for swimming. The wind was cold, too, and the sun hidden behind the clouds most of the day. There was an inch of water on the washroom floor at the campgrounds, so every time we went in, our feet got soaked. And there were more mosquitoes than I had ever seen in my life.

After a couple of days we had had enough. We drove to another lake. This place was also beautiful, but there it rained in torrents. We shivered in our damp tent. Do you know what God said to me when I sulked about our bad fortune? "Think about all you can praise God for and be glad about" (Philippians 4:8, TLB). So, a little reluctantly at first, I began to make a mental list and started to praise God. When I realized how much I had to thank God for and be glad about, our dripping tent did not matter that much. Camping in the rain became fun. (Well, almost!) At least I had a chance to do a lot of reading.

Corrie Ten Boom, in her book *The Hiding Place*, coauthored by John and Elizabeth Sherrill, gives a beautiful illustration of giving thanks in everything. Corrie and her sister, Betsie, of Holland, had been imprisoned by the Germans during World War II for hiding Jews in their home. After a sampling of several prisons, they were finally brought to the dreaded prison camp at Ravensbruck. Corrie's heart sank when she saw the crowded conditions in the barracks; not beds, but sleeping platforms stacked in tiers of three! Filth! Smells! Fleas! Betsie had learned the secret of seeing God in everything and giving thanks in everything. Here is how Corrie tells it:

" 'Give thanks in all circumstances'! [quoted Betsie]. That's what we can do. We can start right now to thank God for every single thing about this new barracks!"

I stared at her, then around me at the dark, foul-aired room.

"Such as?" I said.

"Such as being assigned here together."

I bit my lip. "Oh, yes, Lord Jesus!"

"Such as what you're holding in your hands."

I looked down at the Bible. "Yes! Thank You, dear Lord, that there was no inspection when we entered here! Thank You for all the women, here in this room, who will meet You in these pages."

"Yes," said Betsie. "Thank You for the very crowding here. Since we're packed so close, that many more will hear!" She looked at me expectantly. "Corrie!" she prodded.

"Oh, all right. Thank You for the jammed, crammed, stuffed, packed, suffocating crowds."

"Thank You," Betsie went on serenely, "for the fleas and for—"

The fleas! This was too much. "Betsie, there's no way even God can make me grateful for a flea."

" 'Give thanks in *all* circumstances,' " she quoted. "It doesn't say, 'in pleasant circumstances.' Fleas are part of this place where God has put us."

And so we stood between tiers of bunks and gave thanks for fleas. But this time I was sure Betsie was wrong.[1]

1. Corrie Ten Boom, *The Hiding Place* (Washington Depot, Conn.: Chosen Books, 1971), pp. 180-81.

Corrie and Betsie went out on their work detail each day, swallowed their meager food rations, and returned to their barracks each night. There the women crowded around for their spiritual food, the only thing that kept them from complete despair in the cruel prison camp. Corrie and Betsie read to them each night from their precious New Testament, the only one in the barracks. Corrie called these services "previews of heaven," as together the suffering women listened to the Word of God.

One thing mystified Corrie and Betsie. Where were the guards? At other prisons they had been forced to worship in secret, risking severe punishment, but here no guard appeared to stop them. Later they found out why. The guards would not set foot into their barracks because of the fleas! Betsie had been right, after all.

I am convinced that God is more pleased with our praise even than with our service for Him. He says, "Sacrifice thank offerings to God. . . . He who sacrifices thank offerings honors me" (Psalm 50:14, 23). The psalmist says, "I will praise God's name in song and glorify him with thanksgiving. This will please the Lord more than an ox, more than a bull with its horns and hoofs" (Psalm 69:30-31). "Let them give thanks to the Lord for his unfailing love. . . . Let them sacrifice thank offerings and tell of his works with songs of joy" (Psalm 107:8, 22).

Psalm 71 is supposedly a psalm for old age, but I found it great for middle age, too, and received much blessing from memorizing it. When I go over it I am struck by the importance of praise. The psalmist uses the words *ever* and *all day long* throughout the psalm in connection with praise. "I will *ever* praise you. . . . My mouth is filled with your praise, declaring your splendor *all day long.*" I am convinced this is God's will for the Christian, and possible by His power. When things go right we can say, "Praise the Lord," and when they go wrong, "Praise the Lord anyway!"

We can praise Him even for our weaknesses. Paul said, "Therefore I will boast all the more gladly about my weaknesses, so that Christ's power may rest on me" (2 Corinthians 12:9). We can find joy in every situation, because we know God uses all things for our good. When we believe this, the power of Christ is released in our lives.

If we practice praise we will not have time left to be depressed. Do you think I am oversimplifying? All I can say is that "seeing God in everything" and "thanking Him for everything" are the twin discoveries that led me out of my dark tunnel. Continuing to praise Him is what keeps me from going back.

If you are depressed, try this simple exercise. Make a list of everything you have to thank God for and be glad about. It will take a while if you are really honest. Then stop and thank Him for each one of these blessings. But that is not all. Make another list of the difficult things in your life, and praise God for each one of them, too. Thank Him for what He is teaching you and for what He is going to do to solve these problems for you. Then make a list of your weaknesses, and praise God that they make you more dependent upon Him and thus a candidate for His strength. Praise the Lord!

At first you may feel only slightly encouraged, but don't give up. Keep thanking and praising, and you will find things changing, because your attitude will change to one of expectancy, optimism, and faith, giving God a chance to work in you and through you.

Try praising! I am positive it will work for you as it has for me!

9

The Grumble Rumble

I always shake my head in disbelief at the grumblings of the Israelites on their journey to the promised land. How *could* they complain like that after God delivered them from their slavery in Egypt, opened the Red Sea for them, and supplied all their needs?

If I look closely, I can see the same thing in my life. God has saved me from the bondage of sin and has given me new life, strength for every day, an eternal hope. Yet, as I take a good look, I see that I, too, am quick to complain. Perhaps it is nothing big, so I do not realize what I am doing. Maybe it is grumbling about the icy North Dakota wind, rain on a day we planned a picnic, a blizzard that makes it necessary for us to cancel a trip. Maybe it is that frustrated feeling when the telephone rings all day or other interruptions keep me from my work. Maybe it is an insidious feeling of self-pity that tells me I have a more difficult lot than anybody else. Maybe it is a restlessness, a desire for change, an inner discontent. Maybe it is the feeling that people are not treating me fairly.

When the Israelites complained against Moses and Aaron and talked about returning to the flesh-pots of Egypt, Moses said, "You are not grumbling against us, but against the Lord" (Exodus 16:8). These words always hit me like a blast of icy wind. When I fuss at my husband or complain about my neighbor, I am really fussing against God. That puts complaining in a little different light, does it not?

God calls complaining "rejecting the Lord" (Numbers 11:20), because it is rebelling against what He plans for us. Complaining is doubting God's love. Moses told the Israelites, "You grumbled in your tents and said, The Lord hates us; so he brought us out of Egypt to deliver us into the hands of the Amorites to destroy us" (Deuteronomy 1:27).

Complaining is also unbelief. Moses told the Israelites, "In spite of this, you did not trust in the Lord your God" (Deuteronomy 1:32). They thought they knew better than He did.

How often I am grumpy and unappreciative in spite of the blessings God showers upon me. How I must grieve Him when I forget to be thankful and praise Him. Paul wrote to the Philippian Christians, "Do everything without complaining or arguing" (Philippians 2:14). That is another choice reminder that has a place over my kitchen sink.

Complaining is the twin of self-pity, the most crippling disease known to man. People have conquered diseases such as paralysis, blindness, and leprosy and lived happy, useful lives—but not until they first conquered self-pity.

My oldest sister, Mabel, who has nearly finished rearing twelve children, tells of one of her experiences with self-pity. Recently she wanted very much to attend a Bible conference in another city but offered to baby-sit so others could go. Although she really wanted to be helpful, she felt put upon when a young couple gladly left their two young children with her. The baby's crying and the small boy's incessant chatter combined with her inner discontent to nearly drive her out of her mind. After four days of misery she could stand it no longer and confessed her self-pity to the Lord as the sin that it was. Peace and joy replaced the discontent. The rest of her week of baby-sitting was not only endurable but actually filled with joy.

If you have trouble with self-pity, as I often do, read *Handicap Race*, by Dorothy Clarke Wilson. The story of Roger Arnett's battle against handicaps will make your problems seem small. College track star Roger Arnett was paralyzed from his waist down as the result of a car accident. Self-pity threatened when his fiancée broke their engagement, but he did not allow it to take over. Roger Arnett not only finished college in his wheel chair, but also he found a job as an accountant, married, and adopted three children. Later he supported his family by raising and selling gladioli. When middle-aged, he came to the conclusion that he had been living only for himself and his family and determined to start to do something for others. He became a chaplain to the handicapped and forgotten. Imagine the influence of this man who did his counseling from a wheel chair! Hundreds of lonely, frustrated people looked forward to his encouraging visits. But none of this would have been possible had he not first conquered self-pity.

There is a certain pleasure in feeling sorry for

ourselves, a morbid pleasure to be sure but appealing to our human nature. A woman who recently lost her son in a motorcycle accident said to a friend, "Sometimes I *choose* to suffer. I know that if I go to my room and open my Bible I will find comfort and peace, but I don't always want to."

It's a paradox, is it not, that we enjoy being miserable? Of course it is not true enjoyment, and it has an adverse effect on the person who indulges in it. Not only is he unhappy but he makes his associates and family unhappy as well.

Blind Fanny Crosby, beloved hymn-writer, wrote the following poem when she was nine years old.

Oh what a happy soul I am, although I cannot see;
I am resolved that in this world contented I will be.
How many blessings I enjoy that other people don't!
To weep and sigh because I'm blind, I cannot and I won't!

Mrs. Alice Bretz became blind in late middle age. Shortly afterward, her husband died, leaving her to make difficult adjustments alone. Her story, as told in *I Begin Again,* is a chronicle of courage. She writes: "The stony path is narrow but that brings the wayside flowers closer and their fragrance helps me on my way. Sometimes it rains and the flowers are bruised and beaten to the ground, but then there is the good smell of the wet earth. The rain may sting my face but it doesn't scald like tears of self-pity."[1]

Words like that make me feel ashamed for ever feeling sorry for myself and complaining. I have come to look upon self-pity as one of my deadliest

1. Alice Bretz, *I Begin Again* (Dubuque, Iowa: Finch, 1940), p. 157.

enemies, one that I should shun as I would the plague. The word *devastating* graphically describes its influence upon us.

Darlene Huber was left a widow with six children and a farm to manage when she was just thirty-five. Even though she goes through times of loneliness and frustration, she refuses to indulge in self-pity. When tempted to depression she reads the Psalms. As she reads the heart cries of the psalmist, cries so like her own, she looks to God as the source of her joy, as did the psalmist. Soon she is rejoicing. One of the secrets of her strength is that she believes with all her heart that God not only permitted her husband's death but also planned it; and if it is part of His plan, it has to be good, acceptable, and perfect.

If we really believe that God has a wonderful plan for us that He is gradually working out, we will not indulge in self-pity, no matter what happens. If something is of God (and we can be sure He has permitted it), it is good, for He does all things for our profit.

Would you believe that although everything looks pretty dark at the moment, He has some wonderful surprises ahead for you?

10

Everything Is Against Me

What made Jacob say these doleful words, "Everything is against me"? His sons came back from Egypt, where they had gone to buy corn, and announced that not only had the ruler of the land imprisoned Simeon but also he had demanded that when they came again they bring Benjamin with them.

Jacob could see only tragedy and personal loss. Little did he realize he was on the very threshold of a great joy, that of being reunited with his long-lost son, Joseph.

Job uttered similar words when he lost his riches, his children, and his health: "Remember, O God, that my life is but a breath; my eyes will never see happiness again (Job 7:7). Job's comforters did little to cheer the stricken man, but one of them gave an accurate prediction of Job's future. "He [God] will yet fill your mouth with laughter [Job] and your lips with shouts of joy" (Job 8:21). And so it happened. Job did not stay scraping his sores in the ashes. God restored his health, his family, and his riches. He ended up with twice what he had had in the beginning. "The Lord blessed the latter part of Job's life more than the first" (Job 42:12).

Naomi, too, felt that all was lost when her husband and two sons died leaving her with her widowed daughters-in-law in a strange land. When she returned with Ruth to her hometown, Bethlehem, she told her old friends, "Don't call me Naomi [pleasant], . . . Call me Mara [bitter], because the Almighty has made my life very bitter" (Ruth 1:20). But God had much "pleasantness" yet in store for Naomi. He led Ruth to glean in the field of wealthy, godly Boaz, who eventually became her husband. Naomi not only had all of her financial needs supplied through this marriage, but also her emotional needs; she became a busy, happy grandmother. Life did indeed become pleasant for Naomi, contrary to her expectations.

Elijah also came to the end of his rope. He had seen God work one miracle after another, but later, with Jezebel after him, he became discouraged to the point of wanting to die. "I have had enough, Lord, . . . Take my life," he said in dejection as he sat under the juniper tree (1 Kings 19:4). But God had better plans for Elijah, which included a trip to heaven without dying. Can you imagine the breathtaking splendor of those chariots of fire that came for Elijah? What he would have missed had God answered his prayer of despondency! He would never have prayed that way had he known what glorious plans God had for him.

Have you ever felt as Jacob, Job, Naomi, and Elijah did? "Everything is against me"; "my eyes will never see happiness again"; "Call me Mara, because the Almighty has made my life very bitter"; "Lord

. . . take my life." That is how I felt during my tunnel days. All seemed lost. There was nothing left to live for.

But I found out that God had some surprises around the corner for me, just as He had for these four friends. He has for you, too. He gave me a song for my sob, and He can do the same for you.

One of my favorite Bible passages is 1 Corinthians 3:21-23: "All things are yours, whether . . . the world or life or death or the present or the future—all are yours, and you are of Christ, and Christ is of God." *The Living Bible* puts it this way: "He has given you the whole world to use, and life and even death are your servants. He has given you all of the present and all of the future. All are yours, and you belong to Christ, and Christ is God's."

How can you lose? Do not despair. Trust Him. Praise Him.

11

Calling Card of the Devil

According to an old story, God called Satan to heaven one day to take away his tools with which he wielded power over mankind. Satan was willing to give up all his tools but one—discouragement. This he begged to keep, for with this tool he could wedge an opening into men's lives and eventually bring in all his other evils.

Gladys Hunt in her book *Ms Means Myself* lists the five *d's* of Satan's strategy: disappointment, disillusionment, discouragement, dejection, defeat.

The devil's "d's" stalked John Howard in the sixteenth century. He had just buried his young wife and was on his way to Portugal to help victims of a devastating earthquake, when the ship he was sailing on was seized by a French privateer. John Howard was thrown into a filthy prison in the hold of the ship. Suffering in the dark, dank prison, he began to wonder about other prisons. Did all prisoners fare so badly? When released, he instituted a program of prison reforms from England to Russia. Without his disappointment and the frustration of his plans, perhaps he would never have found the life ministry God had for him.

When disappointments come to us, if we recognize them as "His appointments" we need not descend into disillusionment. What is disillusionment but doubt of God's love and wisdom? If we take our disappointments as part of God's plan for us, we can avoid devastating discouragement. Here is where faith comes in. This is seeing God in everything.

Martin Luther suffered from discouragement, too. In the twelve years after he nailed his famous ninety-five theses to the cathedral door in Wittenberg, he had accomplished great things; he had held his debate with Dr. John Eck, translated the Bible into the common language of the average German, and written many books and hymns. In spite of this, Luther became discouraged.

He tried to shake it off by eating, drinking, and singing with his friends, but this did not help. Finally, in despair when the depression would not leave him, he cried out, "My God, my God, why hast thou forsaken me?" In that instant he found his answer. God! He must look to God, who is the Christian's help in trouble. As Luther looked to God in faith, discouragement fled. Using Psalm 46 as a basis, he wrote the soul-stirring song of the Reformation, "A Mighty Fortress Is Our God."

The psalmist, too, was discouraged. "Why are you downcast, O my soul?" he asked. "My soul is downcast within me; therefore I will remember you" (Psalm 42:5-6). In another instance he said, "My flesh and my heart may fail, but God is the strength of my heart and my portion forever" (Psalm 73:26).

Turning our hearts and thoughts to God is the answer. Remember God: what He has done in the past; what He has in store for us in the future; what He is able to do for us right now.

I visited two dear women of God in a rest home some time ago. "What do you do when discouraged?" I asked one, who always had a smile on her face, despite her aches and pains.

"I go to see what my Lord has to say about it," she answered, "and even if I don't feel any different right away, if He says it, I know everything is OK."

Another woman, almost totally blind, was tempted to discouragement when she woke up in the middle of the night and could not sleep. Her solution? "I quote all the Bible verses I can remember, and the hymns," she said. She repeated for us the comforting words of the hymn written by William O. Cushing, "Under His Wings."

> Under His wings I am safely abiding,
> Tho' the night deepens and tempests are wild,
> Still I can trust Him; I know He will keep me;
> He has redeemed me, and I am His child!

A young university graduate confided that before he came to know Christ he had only one solution for discouragement, a drinking party with the guys. Now he turns to his Bible and fellowship with other Christians.

In the book *Games People Play,* author Eric Berne tells us about the game he calls "Ain't It Awful!" I think Christians are particularly fond of this game, even if it does nothing to lift anybody's spirits. We talk about the drug problem, the immorality, crime, rising prices, pollution, shortages, apostasy, indifferences of Christians, international crises. Ain't it awful!

Certainly it is awful. As Christians and responsible citizens we must do our part to try to curb these evils. Action we need. Endless talk we do not need! Nobody benefits from the "Ain't It Awful!" game.

The Bible tells us to edify one another. Proverbs is full of advice concerning our talk. Here is just a sample: "The tongue that brings healing is a tree of life, but a deceitful tongue crushes the spirit" (Proverbs 15:4); "An anxious heart weighs a man down, but a kind word cheers him up (Proverbs 12:25).

Let's talk about what *God* does in these days, not only here in our country but also all over the world. Let us thank Him for the unprecedented spread of the gospel in our country these days as well as in other parts of the world through television and radio. Let us thank Him for earnest Christian young people witnessing on college campuses and preparing for missionary work abroad. Let us praise Him for godly older people who spend much time in prayer for the younger generations. Let us rejoice in the spiritual hunger evident in communist countries. We do not need to be surprised at the condition of our world. Jesus told us what it would be like in the last days before His return. He also said, "When these things begin to take place, stand up and lift up your heads, because your redemption is drawing near" (Luke 21:28). Let's talk about the second coming of Christ and the reign of righteousness and peace that He is soon to establish.

Discouragement is like measles—catching. That is why God told the fearful and fainthearted Israelite soldiers not to go to battle "so that his brothers will not become disheartened too" (Deuteronomy 20:8). On the other hand, courage and hopefulness are catching as well. I cannot forget Bruce, a member of the Navigator organization, who visited us a few years ago. He was such a happy Christian and so *excited* about living for Christ that we became excited, too. We caught his enthusiasm.

Encouragement is one of the gifts Paul speaks of along with the gifts of preaching and teaching. "And if our gift be the stimulating of the faith of others let us set ourselves to it" (Romans 12:8, Phillips*). What a ministry for us in these days!

There is a legend about a man who found an old barn where Satan kept his seeds to sow in human hearts. The seeds of discouragement were more plentiful than any other, since they could be made to grow almost anywhere. "There is just one place they cannot grow," Satan admitted. "That is in a grateful heart."

So we come right back to praise. Praise and discouragement cannot coexist. "It is good to praise the Lord and make music to your name, O Most High, to proclaim your love in the morning and your faithfulness at night" (Psalm 92:1-3).

---

*J. B. Phillips, *The New Testament in Modern English*.

12
What About Diet?

After I gave my testimony one afternoon at a Christian Women's Club luncheon, an attractive woman came up to speak to me. She, too, had suffered from "nerves," she said, but had found help in a book on diet. The book maintains, she told me, that because people are not getting the proper vitamins, especially vitamin B, they become nervous. Some day I am going to read that book. I am all for vitamins and good health. I believe God wants us to take care of our bodies. However, I have found that even more important than what I put into my stomach is what I put into my mind.

I confess that I am prejudiced against the one-eyed monster that has taken over so many homes today. Perhaps I am too prejudiced even to discuss it objectively. Although television can keep us abreast of world events, serve as innocent entertainment, and even occasionally inspire, I believe that more often it becomes a tool of Satan. I will let the experts discuss its detrimental influence on children and will say only that I have seen its deadening effect on adults—Christian adults. We become used to sinful

things. Even if we avoid the sinful, we become cap-
tivated by things of the world. As one new Christian
told me recently, "If I watch a movie on TV, I'm too
tired to read my Bible afterward. I have to turn off
the TV before the movie starts. Then I get something
out of my Bible."

I believe we underestimate the influence of what
our minds take in day after day. Some filth we cannot avoid, especially on certain jobs where we work
closely with other people whose standards differ
drastically from ours. But much of it we can avoid,
if we try. We can also counteract it by filling our
minds with what is pure and good. One young man
said he felt so contaminated after working at his job
all day that the first thing he did when he got home
was to read several chapters in the Bible. He was too
tired to get much out of them at that time of day,
but by reading the Word he felt his mind cleansed
from the filth he had encountered on the job.

Not only what we see and hear influences us but
also what we read. We *become* what we read. If we
read the newspaper more than we read the Bible we
will likely be anxious, worried people. If we read
secular books and magazines more than Christian
ones we will find ourselves thinking more like un-
believers than like Christians. I cannot say enough
in favor of reading the Bible and good, Christian
books. Of course the Bible must take first place.
When the preacher came to one home and wanted to
read a few verses from the Bible with the family, the
mother said to her little son, "Johnny, run and get the
book that Mother loves so much." The little boy
came back with the Sears catalog.

Reading the Bible every day makes such a difference in my life. As I read God's Word I find prom-

ises to buoy my spirits and evidences of God's power. I see God's plan being worked out not only through the nations and their rulers but also through ordinary men and women in the everyday matters of life. I read of the glorious future for the child of God. I am challenged, rebuked, encouraged, and uplifted. My faith grows. Spiritual things become important. I store up trust thoughts that will come to my rescue when I am tempted to worry and fear.

Some people read the Bible at random, here and there. I prefer to read it systematically from beginning to end. My Bible-reading diet consists of some Old Testament and some New Testament every morning. Psalms are my "bedtime snack." Some people shy away from the Old Testament because of the genealogies. I don't let them bother me; sometimes I skim them, and sometimes I skip them. Because I have found precious treasures in the Old Testament, I read it as much as the New Testament.

I also try to memorize choice chapters, usually from the New Testament or Psalms, spending only about five or ten minutes a day on this but gaining much from it. As I go over the same verses again and again in an effort to commit them to memory, I see truths that were hidden to me when I read casually. My memorizing turns into meditation.

Sometimes I read a piece from a devotional book like *Streams in the Desert,* by Mrs. Charles Cowman, along with my Bible. What a feast it all turns out to be! If I am discouraged when I start, I certainly am not by the time I finish.

I like to read my Bible with pen in hand to mark especially meaningful verses and jot things in the margins. Writing comments in a notebook, which I call my "spiritual journal," has also proved helpful. When I put into words what God has said to me and write it down, somehow it means more. If you tend to be sleepy during Bible reading or are bothered with wandering thoughts, jotting things in a notebook will help to keep you alert, and you will get more out of what you read.

Sometimes I use a concordance and pursue a topic such as faith or repentance, searching out all the references on that particular subject. This also can be a great blessing.

If you are in a rut in your Bible reading, try reading it in another version. One of the modern versions will be easy to understand and helpful. My friend Molly became so interested in reading the book of Joshua in her *Living Bible* that she let her stew burn.

Although the Bible must come first in a Christian's life, other Christian books are also invaluable, especially accounts of other Christians' experiences. "Why, she's just like me!" I gasp in surprise. "I thought I was the only one with that problem!" I have received help, inspiration, and encouragement time and time again from Christian biographies and devotional books. I also become inspired when I read about handicapped people who have triumphed over great obstacles.

You say you do not have time to read? I realize we live in a hectic world these days, and all of us are affected; but we *make* time for what we want to do, what we consider important. We usually take time to eat, no matter how busy we are. Is feeding the soul and mind less important? Should we not also discipline ourselves and make time for that?

I read books mostly in ten- or fifteen-minute snatches—between putting potatoes on to boil and making the salad, or while I stir the pudding. I also usually take a book along when I go anywhere by car. I used to become so impatient when my husband disappeared under the hood. Now I just take out my book and read a few pages. This way I do not mind the delay, because I get quite a number of books read.

My sister, Marion, said to me the other day, "Isn't it a privilege to be able to read in a few hours what has taken someone years to learn and write about?" I had not thought about it that way before, but it certainly is a privilege, isn't it? Just think of the riches waiting for us if we will only take the time to discover them.

Here are some of my favorite books. Some can be found at your public library, others at your Christian bookstore. They are a gold mine of encouragement and inspiration. As you read these and the many others that are available, your life will be enriched, as mine has been.

Brother Andrew, John Sherrill, and Elizabeth Sherrill. *God's Smuggler.* Old Tappan, N.J.: Revell, 1968.

Paul E. Billheimer. *Don't Waste Your Sorrows.* Fort Washington, Pa.: CLC, 1977.

Amy Carmichael. *Mimosa.* Fort Washington, Pa.: CLC, 1958.

Mrs. Charles Cowman. *Streams in the Desert.* Los Angeles: Oriental Missionary Society, 1925.

Richard J. Foster. *Celebration of Discipline.* New York: Nelson, 1984.

John Edmund Haggai. *How to Win Over Worry.* Grand Rapids: Zondervan, 1967.

Frances Gardner Hunter. *PTLA: Praise the Lord Anyway.* Anderson, Ind.: Warner, 1972.

E. Stanley Jones. *The Divine Yes.* Nashville: Abingdon, 1975.

Isobel Kuhn. *In the Arena.* Chicago: Moody, 1968.

Tim La Haye. *Spirit-Controlled Temperament.* Wheaton, Ill.: Tyndale, 1966.

Gordon MacDonald. *Ordering Your Private World.* Nashville: Nelson, 1984.

Catherine Marshall. *Beyond Ourselves.* New York: McGraw-Hill, 1961.

S. I. McMillan. *None of These Diseases.* Old Tappan, N.J.: Revell, 1963.

Keith Miller. *The Taste of New Wine.* Waco, Texas: Word, 1965.

Francis Schaeffer. *True Spirituality.* Wheaton, Ill.: Tyndale, 1971.

Hannah Whitall Smith. *The Christian's Secret of a Happy Life.* Old Tappan, N.J.: Revell, 1888, 1916, 1968.

———. *The God of All Comfort.* Chicago: Moody, 1956.

Corrie Ten Boom and Elizabeth Sherrill. *The Hiding Place.* Edited by John Sherrill. Washington Depot, Conn.: Chosen Books, 1971.

W. Ian Thomas. *The Saving Life of Christ.* Grand Rapids: Zondervan, 1961.

Dorothy Clarke Wilson. *Handicap Race: The Inspiring Story of Roger Arnett.* New York: McGraw-Hill, 1967.

Sabina Wurmbrand. *Pastor's Wife.* New York: John Day, 1971.

13

Too Busy or Too Lazy?

A psychologist friend once told me that depression is really only an escape from reality. When the pressures of real life become too intense to bear, a person escapes by retreating into depression.

I believe this was true in my case. I remember going to our family doctor some months before my breakdown; I was very upset and nervous. When he inquired about my activities I admitted that I had either been out or had company ten evenings running, all in connection with our church work. He was almost angry when he heard this and said that such busyness had to stop. I should have at least two or three nights a week to myself for relaxation.

Some of us are inclined towards busyness. We like to be doing. When the devil cannot stop a person, he gets behind and pushes him to excesses. This is often true in Christian work. We can become so busy and involved that the burdens become too great. It is impossible to face them any longer. A retreat into depression seems the only way out.

A friend of mine has a paper marked with a large *NO* pinned beside her telephone. It had been too easy to say yes to every request that came her way, and she found herself too busy and consequently frustrated. The *NO* reminds her to think twice before she agrees to take on an extra job.

On the other hand, some people are inclined to laziness. They would just as soon drop out of everything and let someone else do it. This is true especially when a woman begins her menopause and does not feel up to par, physically or emotionally. Satan tries to capitalize on this also by making such a person retreat from an active life, giving her too much time to ponder her problems and feel sorry for herself. He is delighted when we go to either extreme—busyness or laziness.

Some years ago a friend remarked, "It's wonderful to see the middle-agers in your church so active. In my church, when a person hits forty he thinks he should be through with his church responsibilities and let younger people take over." Yet, younger people are usually weighed down with many more family responsibilities than middle-agers. Besides, those who have lived forty or fifty years have had more time to learn what life is all about. Now at last we have something to share with others. Shall we drop out—keep it all to ourselves?

No matter what the size of the church, nearly everywhere you go you hear the same lament, "We don't have enough workers for Sunday school, Pioneer Girls, Christian Service Brigade, or choir."

I always received a blessing from reading in Nehemiah 3 about the exiled Israelites, returned from Babylon, rebuilding the wall of Jerusalem. What a gigantic task for the comparatively small band of people to accomplish. But accomplish it they did!

How? By each one doing his share. Read how one group built the sheep gate, unto the tower of Hananeel; another the fish gate, laying the beams and setting up the doors, locks, and bars. Next to them another family built. With each one doing his share, the great task of building the wall was successfully completed.

This is the way it should be in our churches, too: the overly ambitious ones not doing too much, thus becoming exhausted and ultimately depressed; those inclined toward laziness not dropping out completely to ultimately feel useless and unfulfilled; but each one "building his part of the wall" in the kingdom of God.

I am learning to shun both over-busyness and laziness. Both lead to depression. Both are a victory for our enemy.

14

Everybody Needs a Project

I find that having projects has an effect upon my emotional and mental well-being. Daily goals as well as long-range ones are good for us. Maybe my goal for a certain day will be to clean a closet or straighten some drawers besides my routine tasks that must be done. Maybe I will decide to try a new recipe or bake bread for my family. Maybe my goal will be to have friends in for coffee or for a meal. Or I might set out to accomplish a definite amount of writing or typing.

You may have different goals: clean the garage, paint a room, sew a dress, lose weight, put your snapshots in albums. Projects such as these keep us from boredom and depression. Accomplishing something, even a small task, is therapy for our minds and spirits.

Although this type of activity is good and necessary, there is another kind that is even more satisfying—projects that help to build the kingdom of God. Jesus says in John 15:11, "I have told you this so that my joy may be in you and that your joy may be complete." What was the joy of Jesus? To do His

Father's will and to bring many sons unto glory. A speaker at a mission conference in expounding this text remarked, "Jesus wants us to share this joy of being involved in a spiritual, life-giving work. It is deeply satisfying to invest your time, money, and prayers into projects that go on into eternity." We can work on these projects until the day we leave this earth. Age, poverty, disability, nothing need limit us.

To be involved in building the kingdom of God is immensely rewarding. A friend of mine, going through her menopause, suffered from depression. She had crying jags, snapped at her husband and children, and felt that life had become an intolerable burden rather than a joy. She thought that resting from all of her activities outside of her home for a year would help. It did not. Finally she became involved in a Bible study program and opened her home for a Bible class. Gradually, as she became involved in inviting neighbors to the class and studying the Bible with them, her depression lessened. She was engaged in the most exciting business in the world, that of building the kingdom of God! Life took on new meaning and purpose.

During World War II I worked for several months in a defense plant to earn money for Bible school. My work was to tape tanks. After I learned the procedure I could do it automatically, without even thinking. Working eight hours a day at a job that held no challenge for me became extremely boring. I hated going to the plant. Even though I was helping the war effort, I detested the job. I believe we are depressed and restless many times because our jobs are not big enough for us. You may have a very important job such as teaching, homemaking, nursing. Maybe you are an engineer, an executive, or have a business of your own. But sometimes it all seems so futile; what do you really accomplish?

We must remember that our real job is getting to know God and becoming a vital part in building His kingdom, a glorious task that extends to eternity. It is a job that makes use of all of our abilities and potential. If we will, we can accomplish this at the same time we pursue our necessary daily activities. A woman once remarked to a friend, "My house and garden—that's my life." I pity the woman. Think of spending all of her energies on a house and garden that will one day pass away. There is so much more! Pray that God will lead you to the project(s) He has in mind for you.

A young Christian mother in our city took as a project a Korean woman who was new in our town. Mi-yung had not been in the United States for very many months. She could neither speak nor understand English well, had no friends, was bewildered and lonely. Her American husband worked evenings as well as days to supplement their income. Mi-yung spent lonely hours walking the floor with her new baby and crying her heart out. Then Cathy came on the scene. She became Mi-yung's true friend. She took her shopping and taught her American ways. She had her over for coffee and fixed her hair. Sometimes she simply dropped in for a chat and helped her with her English. Gradually Mi-yung stopped feeling so homesick for Korea. She began to like America. She decided to come to a Bible study for Oriental women and learn about God. She began to smile and laugh. Her whole outlook on life changed, all because Cathy had a project, a worthwhile one.

Another Korean girl who moved to our city confided that, although she had lived in the United States for two years, she had never been visited by an American or been invited to an American home. (How many other foreign people in our country receive the same cold-shoulder treatment?) She was delighted when we became friends with her. She, too, was eager to study the Bible after she had experienced true friendship.

A number of Christian women in a small Iowa town took as their project a lonely Japanese war bride, the only foreigner in town. One of them obtained a Japanese Bible for her, gave her and her children rides to church, and helped them celebrate birthdays and other special occasions. Another taught her how to make pie and bread. Another studied the Bible with her on Saturday mornings. Others invited her to their homes for coffee or meals. The result? Toshiko came to faith in Jesus Christ.

What about foreign students in your town, professional people from other countries, migrant workers? What about your neighbor who does not know Christ? What about the young woman down the street who would go to a Bible study if someone would babysit for her? What about the girl in your block who is a bit odd and has no friends? What about the woman who lost her husband recently and is having a difficult time adjusting to life alone? What about that old man in the rest home who never has any company? What about the orphan who needs a foster parent?

There are endless possibilities for projects. The interesting result is that in brightening the lives of others we brighten our own. As Solomon put it in

Proverbs 11:25, "he who refreshes others will himself be refreshed."

Perhaps the greatest project of all is prayer. When we were home on furlough from Japan, Pearl Stevens, a widow with grown children, offered to be our prayer partner. As we returned to the mission field we shared our burdens with this woman who had taken us as one of her projects. Mrs. Stevens prayed especially for our friend Sumiko San, a young woman suffering from tuberculosis in a local hospital in Sakata City. She also sent cards to Sumiko San and wrote little messages of cheer. Sumiko San was so encouraged and blessed by this kindness that she spent hours crocheting doilies to send to Mrs. Stevens to show her appreciation. Shortly after she sent the doilies, Sumiko San went to be with the Lord. When Mrs. Stevens received the doilies she was in the hospital with cancer and passed away shortly afterwards. I like to imagine the meeting of Sumiko San and Mrs. Stevens in the other world and the joy they must have experienced. What a beautiful project for Mrs. Stevens's last days on earth, a project that reached into eternity!

Maybe you would like to take on a similar project. Ask God to show you which missionary family to choose. Write to them often. Send them gifts when you can: a new book, an inspiring gospel record, a box of chocolates, or a game for the children. Ask them to share their prayer burdens with you. Pray specifically for their prayer requests. You have no idea what eternal blessing will result from such a project and at the same time how much you will be blessed.

God has left us here on earth to learn to know

Him, to pray for others, to show His love to others, to prove to the world that He is real, to build His kingdom. What a joy to be a part of this eternal plan!

Depression and boredom are bedfellows. But you do not have to be bored. There are abundant projects waiting for you—projects of eternal value. I am glad I am involved in a few. You can be, too.

15

There Is Treasure in Trouble

During my tunnel days I thought much about the suffering in the world. It was hard to understand how a loving God could allow it. One day I recalled the words of L. E. Maxwell of Prairie Bible Institute: "Suffering is better than sin." I did not really understand those words when I attended Prairie, but I am beginning to now. Floods, fires, wars, catastrophes of all kinds that destroy the body and its comforts are better than sin, which ultimately destroys the soul. God uses these evils to bring people to Himself and eternal hope. A person might lose his house in a flood but through this disaster come home to God.

God says through the prophet Isaiah, "I form the light and create darkness, I bring prosperity and create disaster; I, the Lord, do all these things" (Isaiah 45:7). The prophet Amos brought this message to Israel: "When disaster comes to a city, has not the Lord caused it? . . . 'I gave you empty stomachs in every city and lack of bread in every town, yet you have not returned to me.' . . . 'Many times I struck your gardens and vineyards, I struck them with blight and mildew. Locusts devoured your fig and olive trees, yet you have not returned to me,' declares the Lord" (Amos 3:6; 4:6, 9).

Thank God, some do return; some do find treasure through their trouble. A friend of ours contracted emphysema. It was so severe she had difficulty walking across the room. Before she became ill she had no time for God. "I'm glad I got emphysema," she told a fellow Christian shortly before she died, "because through it I have come to know Christ." Paul said to the Corinthians, "Pain turned you to God" (2 Corinthians 7:9, TLB).

Mr. Yamamoto,* a Japanese cook working for missionaries, had no need for God. He had a beautiful wife, a lovely daughter, a good income, and his sáke bottle. But when his wife ran off with the town Don Juan, Yamamoto's world shattered. Almost simultaneously he contracted tuberculosis and suffered a nervous breakdown. Through this trio of tragedy Yamamoto found God and a wonderful new life. He eventually recovered from his illnesses, got his wife back, and became active in Christian work. He would be the first to admit that there is treasure in trouble. His trouble brought him eternal life. "For God sometimes uses sorrow in our lives to help us turn away from sin and seek eternal life. We should never regret his sending it" (2 Corinthians 7:10, TLB).

God uses trouble. When it comes to us, we would do well to search our hearts and ask, "What is God trying to teach me? Have I grown cold? Have I strayed?" David said, "Before I was afflicted I went astray, but now I obey your word." He went even

*Name has been changed.

further to say, "It was good for me to be afflicted so that I might learn your decrees" (Psalm 119:67, 71).

Troubles make us either bitter or better. A Christian woman testified, "I've never been the same since I lost my little boy. Before that I went to church and all, but somehow God wasn't really important to me. After my little boy died I looked at things with a new perspective."

We are urged throughout the Bible not to resent the chastening of the Lord but to accept it with appreciation. The writer of Hebrews says, " 'My son, do not make light of the Lord's discipline, and do not lose heart when he rebukes you, because the Lord disciplines those he loves, and he punishes everyone he accepts as a son' " (Hebrews 12:5-6). " 'Blessed is the man whom God corrects; so do not despise the discipline of the Almighty. For he wounds, but he also binds up' " (Job 5:17-18*a*). Paul tells the Corinthian Christians, "See what this godly sorrow has produced in you: what earnestness, what eagerness. . . ." (2 Corinthians 7:11). "Sorrow is better than laughter, because a sad face is good for the heart" (Ecclesiastes 7:3).

A friend of mine suffers from a severe case of arthritis. Some nights it has been so painful she has not even gone to bed but has spent the night in a chair. When this affliction came she became very discouraged. *What have I done wrong?* she asked herself. *Why is God punishing me?*

Job asked the same question in his suffering: "Show me where I have been wrong" he cried (Job 6:24*b*). Now, we know that Job's trials were not a punishment for sin. God was so pleased with Job He commended him to Satan as a perfect and upright man who feared God and shunned evil. No,

God was not punishing Job; He was *testing* him.

Neither is God punishing my arthritic friend. He is teaching her things she could never learn apart from suffering. He is training her for some purpose of which she is not aware. Like Job, she can say, " 'But he knows the way that I take; when he has tested me, I will come forth as gold' " (Job 23:10).

Amy Carmichael rescued many children from a life of sin in the temples of India and provided a home for them. This saint who sacrificed so much for others was certainly not free from trouble. During the last eighteen years of her life she was bedridden and suffered a great deal. From her bed she wrote inspiring books that have blessed and challenged Christians all over the world. There was treasure hidden in her trouble.

Problems and difficulties are a necessary part of life: Thomas Edison had 2,500 notebooks filled with facts about problems he was facing.

Problems are not accidental; God has planned them with a purpose in mind. They are the means by which we mature and become conformed to Christ, become usable and prepared for His place for us in eternity. There will be no problems and pressures in heaven to help us grow in faith; only while we are here on earth do we have this opportunity.

James says, "Consider it pure joy, my brothers, whenever you face trials of many kinds, because you know that the testing of your faith develops perseverance. Perseverance must finish its work so that you may be mature and complete, not lacking anything" (James 1:2-4).

George Mueller, who took care of thousands of orphans, looked with delight upon obstacles. He

saw them as opportunities for divine intervention.
The greater the difficulty the better he liked it.

B. H. Pearson said of Mrs. Charles Cowman, author of the much-loved *Streams in the Desert,* "Reverses? To her they are waves to lift her nearer to
God. The swifter the wind blows, the easier to
spread one's spiritual wings and rise heavenward."[1]

One of the treasures I have found in trouble is the
ability to understand and enter into the sufferings of
others. One who has suffered bereavement can help
the newly broken-hearted widow much more than
those who have not experienced bereavement. Having gone through the tunnel of depression I can
empathize with others who are in the same predica-
ment and reach out to them with love and understanding. As Paul says, "Praise be to the God and
Father of our Lord Jesus Christ . . . who comforts us
in all our troubles, so that we can comfort those in
any trouble with the comfort we ourselves have received from God" (2 Corinthians 1:3-4). God uses
trouble not only to teach us, but also to make us
ministers of His comfort to others.

God trusts some of His children with great trials
to prepare them for a special ministry. I know people like that; they are a blessing and spiritual help to
everyone around them because of what God has
taught them through trials.

I overheard two of my sisters talking about the
heartrending experience of being bereaved of children. My older sister lost two babies while serving
as a missionary in Japan, one five days old and the
other a darling eight months. For agonizing months

1. B. H. Pearson, *The Vision Lives* (Fort Washington, Pa.: Christian Literature Crusade, 1961), p. 143.

my younger sister watched her small son die of leukemia.

"I can't explain it," said Marion. "It was so hard and yet so wonderful at the same time. God was so near and precious. I wouldn't trade the experience for anything." And Myrtle agreed.

I feel the same way about my experience in the psychiatric ward and the months of depression that followed. (A different kind of suffering, but suffering nonetheless.) But it was also a blessed learning experience. " 'Who is a teacher like him?' " cried Job in the midst of his suffering (Job 36:22). I echo those words.

Yes, there is treasure in trouble, if we are willing to look for it. Someone has gone so far as to say the worst thing that happens to you can be the best thing that happens to you—if you take it rightly. As the psalmist, it is possible to make our "Valley of Weeping" a well (Psalm 84:6).

Imagine the apostle John's feelings when he was banished to the Isle of Patmos, far away from the Christians he longed to help. But this, too, was part of God's plan. There on the Isle of Patmos John received the wonderful visions that became the "Revelation of Jesus Christ" of our Bible. I doubt we would have had the inspiring classic *Pilgrim's Progress* had John Bunyan not suffered long years of imprisonment for preaching Christ.

Sometimes it is easier to face great, traumatic experiences than small, everyday irritations. But God has a purpose in the little, nagging problems, too. The oyster does not appreciate the gritty grain of sand that lodges between his mantle and shell. But the irritation causes his shell-making glands to produce layer after layer of nacreous shell, which eventually becomes a beautiful, lustrous pearl. Little irritations in our lives, taken rightly, can turn into something beautiful, too. The important thing is our reaction to troubles, whether big or small. If we become resentful towards God and rebel against His dealings with us, we will not find the treasure. It will all be wasted. But if we take it from His loving hands and thank Him for it (in everything give thanks, remember?), our lives will be wonderfully enriched by every problem and calamity that comes our way.

I am amazed whenever I think of our great God, who keeps the planets and stars in their courses and takes so many pains to teach insignificant me. I regret that I have been such a slow learner through the years of my Christian experience. But He never gives up on me, and He will not on you, either. Every day He works with us, teaching, molding, shaping, smoothing off the rough edges, making us like Himself, using whatever means He deems necessary.

But school will soon be over, and there is so much yet to learn!

Ugo Bassi in "Sermon in a Hospital" put it this way:

> If He should call thee from thy cross today,
> Saying, It is finished! the hard cross of thine
> From which thou prayest for deliverance,
> Thinkest thou not some passion of regret
> Would overcome thee? Thou wouldst say, So soon?
> Let me go back, and suffer yet awhile
> More patiently: I have not yet praised God.
>
> (UGO BASSI)

16

A New Chapter in Life's Book

No book on tunnel experiences would be complete without a discussion of bereavement. I cannot write this chapter from personal experience, since I have never lost a close relative, except for my dear father. Daddy was so eager to be with the Lord that I could not grieve when he left us at age eighty-two. But what of those who lose a husband or a wife? Even though they are assured the loved one is with the Lord and they will meet again, how can they adjust to the loneliness and emptiness certain to engulf them?

"Life is never the same again after they are gone," an attractive widow in her sixties told me. In spite of this void in her life, she does not indulge in self-pity. She writes, reads, has friends over, visits her grandchildren, and keeps busy in her church.

Another widow I know keeps so occupied in helping delinquent young people that she has no time to feel lonely, even though she misses her husband very much. A tutor of school dropouts, she has extended her interest to include alienated young people who are searching for reality in life. She invites them to her home, listens to their problems, then tells them of the One who can meet their needs. Her life is full to overflowing.

My mother-in-law takes her loss philosophically. "It would have been so much harder for Dad to be left alone than for me," she says. "I'm thankful God took him first." Now that is positive thinking.

My own dear mother, who was extremely lonely after Daddy died, has made a remarkable adjustment. Even at eighty-three she is active and busy. She has friends in occasionally, as well as reading a great deal and making useful articles for her children, grandchildren, and great-grandchildren.

Life is not the same as before for these widows, but life is still good. They have started a different phase of life and have entered into new experiences.

Naomi thought she had come to the end of all that was good and beautiful, but she found out differently. With her bereavement, a chapter in the book of her life had ended but not the book itself. There were new chapters to write. How carefree and happy Naomi must have felt in her new role as grandmother after her daughter-in-law Ruth remarried and had a son!

A widowed friend of mine constantly sought new occupations to ease her loneliness. She often said, "I think this will be good for me." But the activities she undertook did not seem to fill the void in her life. Gradually she stopped thinking about what would be good for her and began to think about the needs of others. She organized a neighborhood prayer meeting, visited lonely people, opened her home to a college girl. As she became absorbed in the problems of others, her loneliness lessened.

My friend Judy, a special-education teacher, was two years from retirement when her dear husband passed away. She retired from teaching after those two years and now works as a teacher's aide in the special education classes. I asked if the "knife in her heart" was still there after three years of widowhood. "No," Judy said, wiping away a few tears that came to her eyes. "I miss Al so much, but the Lord has healed the hurt. I keep busy at school and church. Life is full and meaningful again."

I was glad to hear her testimony. If God can do that for Judy and these other widows, He can also do it for you, and for me, if we are called upon to face bereavement. If He takes a loved one from me, I must remember to say, "He has done everything well" (Mark 7:37), and praise Him.

17

God Loves Me

The Mano tribespeople of Liberia believe in God as some faraway, impersonal deity. He must be approached through their ancestors and then only in matters of great importance. "God is not interested in a bellyache," they contend.

I disagree. God is interested in *every* part of our lives, the little things as well as the momentous ones. Believing this seems of utmost importance to me.

Yes, God loves us. Sometimes we do not understand why He permits certain difficulties and trials to come to us, but there is where faith comes in—faith in His love. May it never be said of us, "In spite of this, you did not trust in the Lord your God" (Deuteronomy 1:32).

When I was a little girl we said a table prayer that began with the words "God is great, and God is good." Because we ran the words together I thought "godisgreat" was one word and "godisgood" another. I did not have the faintest idea of what they meant. As I grew older, I separated the words to "God is great" and "God is good," but it took me many years to somewhat understand God's greatness and goodness. How important it is that we believe not only in God's greatness but also in His goodness and love.

The telephone rang one Saturday morning when we were still in bed. Our friend Jane was on the line. "I think Bob's dead!" she sobbed.*

We threw on our clothes and hurried to her house. There we found Jane crying and pacing the floor. Her forty-two-year-old husband was lying on the floor. He had suffered a fatal heart attack.

In her extreme grief, Jane at first could not understand why this had happened. She blamed herself for not insisting her husband see a doctor when he had not felt well the day before. Gradually she came to the realization that God had taken her husband. It was not an accident or something she could have prevented. God had done it in His sovereignty. It took longer for the distraught widow to recognize that God had done it *in love.* Only when she came to believe that did she obtain peace.

James Chalmers often said, "As soon as a man comes to understand that God is Love, he is infallibly converted."

F. W. Boreham, in his book *A Handful of Stars,* tells about Dr. Hanley Moule, Bishop of Durham, visiting West Stanley just after a mine disaster. As he faced the relatives of the entombed miners, he told them about an embroidered bookmark, worked in silk, that his mother had given him when he was a boy. The backside was a mass of tangled threads and looked like nothing but a bad mistake; but

---

*Names have been changed.

when he turned it over he saw beautifully embroidered the words GOD IS LOVE. "We are looking at
all this today," he said, "from the wrong side. Some
day we shall see it from another standpoint and
shall understand."[1]

Can we believe in His love even when we do not
understand? The poem "The Weaver" assures us we
can.

> My life is but a weaving
>   Between my Lord and me;
> I cannot choose the colors
>   He worketh steadily.
>
> Ofttimes He weaveth sorrow,
>   And I in foolish pride
> Forget He sees the upper
>   And I, the underside.
>
> Not till the loom is silent
>   And the shuttles cease to fly
> Shall God unroll the canvas
>   And explain the reason why.
>
> The dark threads are as needful
>   In the Weaver's skillful hand
> As the threads of gold and silver
>   In the pattern He has planned.
>
>   (AUTHOR UNKNOWN)

This year was the first time we have ever had a
funeral on the morning of Christmas Eve. Four days
earlier, three girls of our city were hit by a train at

1. F. W. Boreham, *A Handful of Stars* (Philadelphia: Judson, 1922),
p. 115.

an icy crossing. Two were killed instantly and the
third seriously injured. One of those killed was a
member of our church. When the father of the girl
called at two o'clock in the morning to tell us the sad
news, I could not believe what he said. Was I having
a nightmare? It could not be true! Jo Ellen, attractive, intelligent, full of life, energy, and plans for the
future—dead? Impossible!

I could not sleep, so I turned on the light. With
tears streaming down my face, I reached for my
Bible. I opened to the Psalms and read at random,
hungry for some reassurance from the Lord. Everything I read spoke of His mercies, compassion, and
lovingkindness. My anguished "Why, Lord?" turned
to humble gratitude for His love, even though I
could not understand. I prayed that the heartbroken
parents would also be able to believe in His love.

The first thing the weeping mother told me when
I saw her the next day was, "God must have had a
reason." In spite of their crushing sorrow, both parents acknowledged God loved them, that He loved
their daughter whom He took. They believed in His
love, even though they could not understand why
He had permitted the tragedy. They knew God had
allowed the accident to happen for a purpose. Trusting in His love, they found peace and comfort in the
midst of their heartbreak.

There are so many beautiful words in the Bible to
assure us of God's love. "Are not two sparrows sold
for a penny? Yet not one of them will fall to the
ground apart from the will of your Father. And even
the very hairs of your head are all numbered. So
don't be afraid; you are worth more than many
sparrows" (Matthew 10:29-31). "How precious to

me are your thoughts, O God! How vast is the sum of them! Were I to count them, they would outnumber the grains of sand" (Psalm 139:17-18). " 'For I know the plans I have for you,' declares the Lord, 'plans to prosper you and not to harm you, plans to give you hope and a future" (Jeremiah 29:11).

Even in His chastening of us we see His love. He says, " 'My son, do not make light of the Lord's discipline, and do not lose heart when he rebukes you, because the Lord disciplines those he loves, and he punishes everyone he accepts as a son' " (Hebrews 12:5-6).

God loves me. Glorious thought! He thinks about me and plans for my good. It awes me to think He cares that much, but He says He does, and I believe it. No matter what happens, I can trust His love. And so can you.

18

Guard Your Link with God

Our enemy's favorite trick is to lead us into unbelief. If the devil can get us to doubt, he has won a great victory, for there is no way to receive anything from God except through faith. Even God cannot help us if we refuse to believe.

Satan used this trick on the first human being he ever tempted, Eve. "Did God really say, 'You must not eat from any tree in the garden'? . . . You will surely not die, . . . For God knows that when you eat of it your eyes will be opened, and you will be like God, knowing good and evil" (Genesis 3:1, 4-5). Satan first attacked God's word, tried to make Eve doubt what God had said. Then he subtly attacked God's character. In essence he was telling Eve, "God is depriving you of something that you should have and would greatly enjoy. He doesn't really love you."

Our enemy attacks in the same way today. First he turns our attention away from the promises of God. He makes us forget them completely or doubt they are for us. Then he subtly makes us question God's love. How could He love you and let you suffer like

this? Or, how could He love you and take away
from you something that you treasure so dearly?

Another weapon our enemy uses is the lie that we
know better than God. We are smarter than He is,
and therefore know what is best for us. God says,
" 'For my thoughts are not your thoughts, neither
are your ways my ways,' declares the Lord. 'As the
heavens are higher than the earth, so are my ways
higher than your ways and my thoughts than your
thoughts' " (Isaiah 55:8-9). Paul says, "Oh, the
depth of the riches of the wisdom and knowledge of
God! How unsearchable his judgments, and his
paths beyond tracing out!" (Romans 11:33).

Hindsight is better than foresight. How often
when we look back we can see the wisdom of God's
decisions and actions even though at the time they
seemed all wrong. Cannot we trust Him to do what
is best for us even though we do not understand?
Can we not listen to His reassurances instead of to
the devil's lies?

Job said, "Though he slay me, yet will I hope in
him" (Job 13:15).

Peter said, "These have come so that your faith—
of greater worth than gold, which perishes even
though refined by fire—may be proved genuine and
may result in praise, glory and honor when Jesus
Christ is revealed" (1 Peter 1:7).

Our faith is indeed precious, for it is our link with
God and the hands that receive His blessings. We
may lose material possessions, reputation, home,
family, and freedom, but if we still have our faith in
God we are immeasurably rich. The greater our
faith in the love and wisdom of God, the greater our
peace and happiness. Charles Spurgeon said, "Little

faith will bring your souls to heaven, but great faith will bring heaven to your souls."

Must Jesus say to us as He did to the disciples, "You of little faith . . . why did you doubt?" (Matthew 14:31).

John the Baptist's faith was sorely tempted when he was thrown into prison after he had so faithfully and fearlessly prepared the way for the coming of Jesus. Languishing in prison, he began to doubt. Was Jesus truly the Messiah for whom they had waited? Was He the Christ? He had to know, so he sent two of his disciples to Jesus with the question, "Are you the one who was to come, or should we expect someone else?"

Jesus continued to heal the sick, the lame, and the blind, and cast out evil spirits. Then He told John's disciples to go back and tell John what they had seen and heard. "And tell him, 'Blessed is the one who does not lose his faith in me' " (Luke 7:23, TLB).

He says the same to us in our trials.

"I am still confident of this: I will see the goodness of the Lord in the land of the living" (Psalm 27:13).

19

In Acceptance Lieth Peace

Psychologists tell us that emotional problems in adults often hark back to childhood. As I reminisced, I realized that although I had a happy childhood I did suffer from feelings of inferiority. My sister slightly older than I had dimples and an engaging personality. The one just younger had sparkling eyes, rosy cheeks, and made everybody laugh. I was very ordinary looking and quiet. I vied for attention by being good and working conscientiously at school and home. I remember marveling that my mother loved me (I was sure she did) when I had neither dimples nor rosy cheeks.

Could these childhood feelings of inferiority have anything to do with my problems as an adult? Everyone thought I cracked up from overwork, but what made me overwork? As I thought it over, I concluded that it was my way of seeking acceptance. My feelings of inferiority from my childhood carried over into my adult life. I tried to compensate for these feelings by excelling in other ways, by doing my share of the work of the church and more than my share. I wanted people to approve of me, wanted to approve of myself, and even more than that, I wanted God to approve of me. I shudder when I think of the years I spent building up my own ego, all the while thinking I was building up the kingdom of God. (Let's hope there is a little gold, silver, and precious stones among the wood, hay, and stubble!)

God showed me that behind every inferiority complex, including mine, is a wrong set of values. Television and magazine advertisements of our day contribute to this false philosophy. The world makes much of a pretty face, a youthful figure, sex appeal, athletic prowess, a superior intellect, and material possessions. God makes much of love, joy, peace, faith, patience, kindness, goodness, faithfulness, gentleness, and self-control. Jesus said, "What is highly valued among men is detestable in God's sight" (Luke 16:15).

Sometimes a person with an inferiority complex is harboring hidden bitterness—bitterness against God for making him as he is. Isaiah's words come to mind: "Shall what is formed say to him who formed it, 'He did not make me'?" (Isaiah 29:16). When we complain about the way we are made, we really complain against the wisdom of God. This came as a shock to me. I was also shocked when I realized that my inferiority complex was not humility, as I had supposed, but pride in disguise. I was afraid of being discovered as I really was. Therefore, I had to work very hard to please and impress.

Gradually it dawned on me that I had never really accepted myself. "If God accepts me in Christ as His child," I reasoned, "surely I should be able to accept myself."

A familiar prayer says it so well:

> Lord, grant me the serenity
>   To accept the things I cannot change,
> To change the things I can,
>   And the wisdom to know the difference.

There are some things I can change about myself, traits of disposition displeasing to God and obnoxious to others. With the help of God's Spirit I need daily to work on my tendencies to impatience, anger, frustration, and other manifestations of self. But the things I cannot change, such as the size of my chin and my personality, I must accept. Accepting myself also includes accepting my limitations. How often I have fretted about being high-strung and having neurotic tendencies. I looked at others who could endure so much more noise, commotion, and strain than I. Why could not I have been built with steel nerves like theirs?

A missionary doctor friend of ours explained it this way: "It's like the material we make our clothes from. Some of it is delicate and has to be carefully washed by hand, while some is so sturdy it can stand up to much abuse. God has made each of us different. He has a reason for making some of us weaker than others."

What could the reason be, I wondered. Later I found it in Paul's writing. He, too, had a thorn in the flesh, which God did not remove from him even though Paul asked Him repeatedly to do so. Finally God said to Paul, "My grace is sufficient for you, for my power is made perfect in weakness" (2 Corinthians 12:9). Paul came to see that his thorn was not something to shun and mourn but to be thankful for. Why? Because in his weakness he experienced the power of Christ. He went so far as to say he gloried in the difficulties that came to him. Even though they revealed his weakness, they also revealed the strength of Christ on his behalf and made him depend more on God.

The Bible abounds with illustrations of people who have lost the blessing of God through pride and independence. God wants us to be dependent upon Him. The more dependent we are upon Him, the more He can release His mighty power in our behalf. If limitations accomplish that purpose, they are friends, not foes. We should not only accept them, but also thank God for them. I must accept not only myself and my limitations but also others with their limitations. How many people get married expecting to change their mates, only to discover they will not be changed. The would-be mate-changer becomes frustrated when his plans do not materialize. How much better to accept each other as we are—limitations, idiosyncrasies, and all—and leave the changing to God.

Sometimes we turn sour because we cannot accept the imperfections of life. These imperfections may be in another person, our marriage, the church community, or ourselves. How many marriages fail because one partner or the other is seeking perfection or at least a high standard that cannot be attained.

Francis Schaeffer in his book *True Spirituality* explains the imperfections of life as an inevitable result of the fall of man. "On this side of the fall," he states, "and before Christ comes, we must not insist on 'perfection or nothing' or we will end with the 'nothing.' "[1]

Gladys Hunt in her book *MS Means Myself* has this to say about such an attitude. "Some people are angry at God. Perfectionists often are, even though they won't admit it. Life hasn't been neat and tidy and the way they planned. Anger at God is a symptom. The basic problem is unbelief. God isn't in charge, or if He is, He blew it. . . . Perfectionists want to be God's chief counselors because they don't believe He can do it without them."[2]

We must also accept *circumstances* that we cannot change. How many people have moved to a new town because of a job transfer or some other exigency, only to find that they cannot stand the place? Maybe it is the wife who hates the new home. The climate is unpleasant; the neighbors are not friendly; the churches are cold; nothing is right. Yet it may be necessary to spend a number of years, even many years, in this "hateful" place. What can we do about it? Accept it as from God.

Sometimes we blame our unhappiness on our circumstances and other outward factors. While I was going through my depression I was always looking for greener pastures. If we took a trip, I was sure I'd feel content and happy. I found that I was just as miserable on the trip as I had been before. I then blamed my unhappiness on being away from home and living out of a suitcase. If I could only return to my own home I would not feel depressed. To my

1. Francis Schaeffer, *True Spirituality* (Wheaton, Ill.: Tyndale, 1971), p. 136.
2. Gladys Hunt, *Ms Means Myself* (Grand Rapids: Zondervan, 1972), p. 109.

dismay I found that my depression followed me right back to my home in North Dakota. I failed to realize that my depression was not caused by outward circumstances; it was *within me.* I was the one that needed to change, not my circumstances. Understanding that was a step in the right direction.

Joseph in the Old Testament accepted his circumstances, even if they were far from ideal. Being a slave in Potiphar's house was not part of his dreams; nor was his stint in the dank Egyptian prison. He not only accepted those unpleasant situations, but he capitalized on them. He made the best of his situation to such an extent that Potiphar made him the manager of his household, and the jailer made him his right-hand man.

I realized that I needed to accept my circumstances, the great traumatic changes as well as the little inconsequential irritations of my days. As long as I struggled and rebelled against these things I was depressed and miserable. But as soon as I accepted what I could not change, put it into the hands of God, and praised Him, peace came. To accept everything as from God is not blind resignation to fate as some would think. It is really living by faith, applying faith to every facet of daily life. It is believing God's promise that He makes everything—yes, everything—work together for the good of His children. It is trusting Him to do what we cannot. It is accepting all things, even the unpleasant, from the hand of a loving, all-powerful Father, who is working out a beautiful plan for our lives.

Darlene Huber, North Dakota homemaker and farmer's wife, realized last March that her husband must undergo open-heart surgery. Both she and Harold had become children of God through faith in Jesus Christ some years before and were happy, rejoicing Christians. As they contemplated heart surgery they did so without panic. God would not fail them.

Before surgery at the University of Minnesota Hospital, Darlene, Harold, and their oldest daughter read Scripture together, held hands, and prayed that if it were God's will, the operation would be successful. Then Darlene added, "If it's not Your will, Lord, we will accept it." Darlene had no doubts that God would bring her husband safely through surgery. In the waiting room she was calm and confident, concerned about others who were desperately worried about their loved ones. Her daughter said to her, "Look how worried some of these people are. Isn't it awful not to have faith?"

After her husband had been in surgery for seven hours, Darlene began to feel a little uneasy and went to talk to the doctor. He admitted they were having problems with her husband's blood pressure, but they were trying something new and hoping it would help.

Darlene pressed for more information. "Does he have a fifty-fifty chance?" she asked. The doctor nodded.

A little shaken by this time but still confident that God would work a miracle, Darlene went to a phone and called one of her prayer partners. About an hour later she went in to see the doctor again. He told her they would talk to her in the chapel.

"Is he dead?" she asked.

"No."

"But you don't think he'll make it."

The doctor shook his head.

Darlene felt as if she were going to faint. She reached into her purse for her New Testament. Just holding it in her hand made her feel stronger. She went to the chapel, threw herself down on her knees, and began to beg God to spare her husband. Suddenly she stopped praying. The words she had said that morning came back to her: "If it is not your will, Lord, we will accept it."

Darlene prayed again, this time for forgiveness. She told God she would accept her husband's death, if that was what He had planned for them. As she did this, a wonderful, indescribable peace and warmth flooded her being. She was, as it were, enveloped in the love of God. Later she found out it was the exact moment of her husband's death that she had felt this beautiful warmth and comfort.

Darlene went back to her family of six children and her ranch of seventy head of cattle, confident that God makes no mistakes. It is not easy to manage the farm, but Darlene brings everything to the Lord. Her faith firms up with every answered prayer, whether it is an offer to buy her cattle when she wonders where and when to sell or a friendly neighbor who comes in to help just when she is trying to catch a sick calf to give him a shot. When tempted to feel sorry for herself because she lost her husband while he was still so young, Darlene tells herself, "God did it. Why should I grieve? This is His will for me and my family. He knows what is best."

Catherine Marshall in her book *Beyond Ourselves* points out the difference between resignation and acceptance. Resignation is negative, acceptance positive. It is not resigning ourselves to the inevitable but accepting everything as from a loving Father that brings peace. If we really accept circumstances from Him, we will thank Him for them, too, knowing that they are for our benefit as He has promised.

Hannah Hurnard has written a beautiful allegory of the victorious Christian life entitled *Hinds' Feet on High Places*. The main character, Much-Afraid, longs to escape from her fearing relatives in the Valley of Humiliation to the high places where the Chief Shepherd dwells. When she is at last willing to start on her journey to the high places, the Chief Shepherd gives her two companions, who also serve as guides; their names are Sorrow and Suffering.

At first Much-Afraid shrinks back from them in horror but finally accepts them and finds they are good companions. Their path leads through many difficulties and dangers. Especially disappointing is the desert that Much-Afraid must cross as part of her journey. It is there that she finds one golden flower growing in the desolate wastes. When she asks its name the flower answers, "Acceptance-with-Joy."

Much-Afraid is comforted by the little flower's answer. She sees that her Shepherd has a purpose, even in her desert wanderings. She decides to adopt the name as her own, "Acceptance-with-Joy."

Wouldn't it be a good name for us, too?

Amy Carmichael said, "In acceptance lieth peace!"

20

Only True Basis
for Happiness

I am convinced the reason for some of our depression is that we base our happiness on false premises. The prophet Amos rebuked God's people for rejoicing in a thing of nothing, their own strength. He said, "And just as stupid is your rejoicing in how great you are, when you are less than nothing! And priding yourselves on your own tiny power!" (Amos 6:13, TLB). If we do this, what happens when our strength is gone, when we become ill or disabled by an accident? The basis for our happiness is gone. We become depressed.

Micah, who lived in the time of the judges of Israel, was crushed when fellow Israelites robbed him of his gods and his priest. Pursuing the thieves, he cried out pathetically, "You took the gods I made, and my priest, and went away. What else do I have?" (Judges 18:24). Poor man! Happiness based on what can be lost or stolen is insecurity indeed.

Often we base our happiness on circumstances. If things work out according to our plans, we are happy; if our plans go awry, we become depressed.

Circumstances are subject to sudden change. We may be forced to move, take a different job, care for an invalid relative, or become ill ourselves.

Many times we base our happiness on people. As long as one's husband is kind, the children are good, and friends are loyal, we feel happy. But even the best of husbands sometimes fail, children invariably get into trouble some time or other, and often friends let us down. What then? Some people are so dependent on their loved ones for their happiness that their world goes to pieces when those loved ones leave. Maybe it will be a mate taken away by death. Maybe it will be a child leaving home for school, work, or marriage. Without them life becomes meaningless.

For years I based my happiness on what I could accomplish. True, a job well done brings its own satisfaction. God made us that way. We must have goals, or we will not accomplish much. But this should not be the *basis* for our happiness. If it is, we become frustrated and resentful over the interruptions that keep us from accomplishing our goals, serious things such as accidents and illness, as well as little things, such as unexpected guests, long telephone calls, or flat tires. We must remember that God permits these interruptions as a part of our training in His school.

D. Martyn Lloyd-Jones in his excellent book *Spiritual Depression: Its Cause and Cure* warns against another facet of this very thing. He states, "One of the greatest dangers in the spiritual life is to live on your own activities. In other words, the activity is not in its right place as something which you do,

but has become something that keeps you going."[1]
When illness or old age stops these activities, acute
depression sets in.

A common mistake Christians make is to base
their happiness on their success in the work of the
Lord. We experienced this especially when we were
in Japan. When new people came to church and
received Christ, our joy knew no bounds. When the
national Christians attended services faithfully, wit-
nessed to others, grew spiritually, we floated on
cloud nine. But reverses came. The promising new
"convert" turned out to be a Communist just pre-
tending to be a Christian to get into the church and
cause trouble. For weeks no new seekers came.
Sometimes Christians we had counted on would
backslide. It was very easy to get depressed at times
like these.

Jesus warned His disciples about basing their happiness on their success in His work. The seventy
disciples came back from their first evangelistic trip
elated at their success. They said, " 'Lord, even the
demons submit to us in your name" (Luke 10:17).
Jesus answered, "Do not rejoice that the spirits submit to you, but rejoice that your names are written
in heaven" (Luke 10:20).

"Base your happiness on your hope in Christ,"
says Paul (Romans 12:12, Phillips). This is the only
true basis for our happiness. Everything else is subject to change and disappointment. Throughout the
Bible we are urged to "rejoice in the Lord," to be

---

1. D. Martyn Lloyd-Jones, *Spiritual Depression: Its Cause and Cure*
(Grand Rapids: Eerdmans, 1965), p. 198.

"glad in the Lord." The psalmist affirms over and over again, "The Lord is my portion."

"This is what the Lord says, 'Let not the wise man boast of his wisdom or the strong man boast of his strength or the rich man boast of his riches, but let him who boasts boast about this: *that he understands and knows me'*" (Jeremiah 9:23-24, italics added).

Think of Paul's circumstances. In 2 Corinthians 11 we find a list of his sufferings: hard work, severe floggings, imprisoned frequently, beatings, stonings, shipwrecks, in danger, weariness, painfulness, hunger and thirst, cold, and nakedness. Besides these troubles, he had been forsaken by friends. Yet while the prisoner of wicked Nero, Paul could say, "I have learned to be content whatever the circumstances" (Philippians 4:11). Paul had learned to base his happiness on his relationship with Jesus Christ. He said, "I consider everything a loss compared to the surpassing greatness of knowing Christ Jesus my Lord" (Philippians 3:8).

This is the only true basis for happiness—hope in the unchanging Christ. Martin Luther said, "If we realized what we have in Christ, we'd die for the joy of it."

May we say with the prophet, "Though the fig tree does not bud and there are no grapes on the vines, though the olive crop fails and the fields produce no food, though there are no sheep in the pen and no cattle in the stalls, yet I will rejoice in the Lord, I will be joyful in God my Savior" (Habakkuk 3:17-18).

21
Are You So Foolish?

There was nothing dramatic about my conversion at age five. Some folks probably doubted it was real, but I knew it was. By simple faith I had invited Christ to come into my life, and I was sure He did.

From the time of my conversion I longed to be a "good Christian," one who would accomplish great things for God. I daydreamed about becoming a foreign missionary someday, held "Sunday school" on the front steps at school during noon hour with my sister when I was in the second grade, and faithfully read my Bible every day almost as soon as I learned to read.

Except for a few years during my adolescence, when I was more interested in being accepted by my peers than in anything else, I worked hard at serving God. One day at Bible school, when I was seventeen, I shocked my friends by appearing at breakfast with my hair severely braided and rolled into an unbecoming bun at the nape of my neck. I had been quite vain about my long, blond tresses, and this was my way to show God I was through with frivolity and self. I then proceeded to do the

most difficult thing I could imagine, write my boy-
friend (now my husband) who was serving overseas
in the Navy, a "Dear John" letter. I dumped my dia-
ries, love letters, and pictures in the incinerator behind the dorm and watched them go up in flames. I
thought I had reached the ultimate in consecra-
tion—I was willing to be an old maid for God.

God led otherwise. Seven years later I found myself on a freighter bound for Japan with my husband
and year-old son. My desire to be a foreign missionary was at last realized. During my years in Japan I
tried very hard to be an ideal missionary. I worked
hard at learning the language while caring for my
home and children. When I went to bed at night I
felt as if I were in a forest: the trees were the Japanese words I had been studying during the day. I
could not forget them, even at night. Gradually I
became proficient enough with the language to
work with the Sunday school teachers and with the
women. After about three and a half years of this, I
had a nervous collapse and had to go to the mountains for a six-month rest.

Now, as I look back, I can see that much of my
problem was in depending on myself instead of
upon God. Certainly I knew that I was saved by
faith with no merits of my own, but I was trying to
live the Christian life in my own strength instead of
in the power of the Holy Spirit. Paul could have said
to me as he did to the Galatians, "Are you so foolish?
After beginning with the Spirit, are you now trying
to attain your goal by human effort?" (Galatians
3:3).

I missed the meaning of Colossians 2:6, "Just as

you received Christ Jesus as Lord, continue to live in him." How had I received Him? By faith. But how was I living? By self-effort.

During my six months in the mountains recuperating, and also during our summer vacations there, I heard messages from conference speakers on the fullness of the Holy Spirit. I knew this was what I needed, and I asked God for it. For a few days I was convinced that the Holy Spirit had indeed taken over the controls of my life, but later, when problems came up, I doubted. You see, I had accepted Christ by faith, but when it came to the fullness of the Holy Spirit I went by feelings. The result was an up-and-down Christian life—often down.

I thank God for His patient teaching. Gradually I came to see that I can count on the Holy Spirit's filling me just as I can count on Christ's living in me. By faith I can claim His fullness if I have met the conditions—confessed all known sin and turned over the controls of my life to Him. I realize that the fruit of the Spirit will not ripen in a day. I will not suddenly be filled with perfect love for everyone, unspeakable joy, a meek, longsuffering attitude that will take slights without a murmur. But the Holy Spirit is working these things out in me. The fruit is growing as I yield to Him. I know my joy is increasing as I learn to praise Him in every situation of life.

The rest will come, too, as I yield and obey. But I must claim it—by faith. I have been a doubter too long.

I will have to admit that although I have been a Christian for many years, I am just a beginner when it comes to the Spirit-filled life. Self-effort comes much more naturally to me than complete dependence on the Holy Spirit. But as my button reads: "P B P G I F W M Y"—"Please be patient; God isn't finished with me yet." And He will not be until I see Him face to face.

22

It Must Be a Daily Victory

After what I have written, perhaps you think I have no more troubles with myself and that I go about my daily life with never a down moment, floating about on cloud nine, constantly praising God. No, I have found that a person never arrives once and for all at a point of victory; we must *daily* take the victory that God offers us.

Francis A. Schaeffer in *True Spirituality* states, "All men have psychological problems." He goes on to say, "A person may be healed psychologically, but that does not mean that he will be psychologically perfect the rest of his life."[1] Since I was delivered from my dark tunnel I have never returned to it, thank God. I have, however, had bouts with depression that hit all of us. When things go wrong, when I do not feel up to par, or when the routine of life becomes monotonous, I am tempted to give in to depression and enjoy a few hours of luxurious self-pity.

1. Francis Schaeffer, *True Spirituality* (Wheaton, Ill.: Tyndale, 1971), pp. 132, 134.

But I cannot stay in that condition for long. It reminds me of the tunnel, and I do not want to go near that again. It also smacks of unbelief and ingratitude. After all that God has done for me, how can I grieve Him by indulging in a complaining attitude? Thank God, He has shown me the way out. Even though I do not feel thankful at the moment, by an act of my will I begin to thank God. I deliberately turn my mind from depressing thoughts to happy ones.

One day I felt disgruntled. Things were not going as I had planned. Life was dull. Everything seemed wrong. As I turned to my Bible reading for the day I was startled by these words: "For you have heard my vows, O God; . . . I will ever sing praise to your name and fulfill my vows day after day" (Psalm 61:5, 8). It was a rebuke from heaven itself. What about those vows of mine? I had forgotten all about them. You can be sure I began to praise immediately, and my gloom was forced to leave.

We cannot depend upon former victories. The devil is after us every day to make us fall into one of his favorite traps—gloom and depression. He is always there when we are weary or under stress of some kind. Sensing our weakness he moves in with his powerful forces. We can either defeat him through the power of Christ and go forward to further victories, or we can allow him to defeat us.

One morning after I had been out of the tunnel for several years, I awakened with a splitting headache and the urge to cry. I had been under a severe strain the day before, and now it was catching up with me. I tried to thank God but could only cry. I was attending a conference at the time and had looked forward to this last day of meetings. But as I looked at myself I knew I could not go to the conference that day. I was too upset. I could not bear to think of going into that crowd of people. What if I started to cry?

"I'll go downstairs and tell our hostess I don't feel well," I decided. "I'll offer to do the dishes and peel the potatoes for dinner. The rest of the time I'll stay in bed." But even contemplating facing our hostess seemed too much. I would probably burst into tears and make a fool of myself. I could not face anyone today. Lying back on the pillow, I pulled the covers up around me. My husband could explain for me.

As I lay there looking forward to a day in bed feeling sorry for myself, I became uneasy. I remembered other days like this, *tunnel* days. Did I want to go back to *that,* even for a day? Did I want to retreat, lose ground that had been taken with such effort? No, no, a thousand times no! I jumped out of bed and dried my tears. Even the ordinary chore of dressing helped me forget about myself. I went downstairs and began to talk to our hostess as we prepared breakfast together. There were no tears. Would you believe that I forgot about my depression until my husband appeared about twenty minutes later and asked me how I felt? I went to the conference that day and gained much spiritual help. It was a "going forward" day. What if I had stayed in bed?

When upset or depressed we need to read God's Word, pray, and praise. That is where our help is—in Him. Then we need to get up and be doing, whatever the task at hand. Moping around is *never* the answer.

It might seem impossible to face the day, but face

it you must, unless you want to retreat in the direction of the tunnel. Remember Paul's words, "I can do everything through him who gives me strength" (Philippians 4:13). As you take the first step in faith, He will come to your rescue and see you through. You might not conquer your depression immediately, but you will be on the road to victory. You will soon be able to *thank* Him instead of feeling sorry for yourself, and find yourself on top again.

Satan is out to defeat us *every* day. Each day we must take the victory Christ offers, *by faith*, the faith that praises Him no matter how we feel. Paul tells us in Romans 8:37, "In all these things we are more than conquerors through him who loved us." What does it mean to be more than a conqueror? It means that we not only gain the victory, but also we gain rich spoil from our enemies. In having gone through the battle and conquered, we become enriched spiritually and experience growth in grace and Christian character. Even battles become beneficial.

"Hallelujah! Thank you, Lord! How good you are! Your love for us continues on forever. Who can ever list the glorious miracles of God? Who can ever praise him half enough?" (Psalm 106:1-2, TLB).

23

A Tunnel or a Pit?

I had not been able to get next to Gloria* until I confided in her that I had gone through a long siege of depression. She perked up at once. "You, too?" she asked in surprise. Evidently some of us are quite adept at covering up. I then went on to tell her about my tunnel experience.

"Tunnel!" she exclaimed. "Be glad that's all it was. Mine is a pit! A bottomless one!" For over ten years Gloria, attractive, wealthy, and the mother of a lovely family, had suffered, not in a dark tunnel, but in an indescribable pit from which there was no escape.

My heart went out to Gloria. I tried to analyze why her suffering had been so much worse than mine. I came to the conclusion it was because, although she was seeking God, she did not have the assurance that He had accepted her. If I had not known that I was God's child through personal faith in Christ, my tunnel, too, would have been a pit. Knowing Jesus Christ personally made the differ-

*Name has been changed.

ence. Even in my blackest moments I knew He was there, holding me, loving me, caring for me. I knew I had heaven waiting for me, no matter what happened.

I did not earn this assurance by any efforts of my own. I simply received what God offered me, the gift of His Son, to be my Savior from sin and Lord of my life. As I mentioned, I was only five years old when I made this transaction with God. Maybe you scoff at such an idea. "How could a five-year-old child understand enough to enter into an experience of salvation?" you ask.

A great deal of understanding is not required. Only faith and a willingness to accept what God has provided—His Son. Jesus said, " 'Anyone who will not receive the kingdom of God like a little child will never enter it' " (Luke 18:17).

There are four things you must know:

1. God loves you: "For God so loved the world that he gave his one and only Son, that whoever believes in him shall not perish but have eternal life" (John 3:16).

2. Sin has separated you from God: "For all have sinned and fall short of the glory of God" (Romans 3:23). "For the wages of sin is death, but the gift of God is eternal life in Jesus Christ our Lord" (Romans 6:23).

3. Christ died to pay the price for your sin: "But God demonstrates his own love for us in this: While we were still sinners, Christ died for us" (Romans 5:8).

4. You must receive Him by a simple act of your will, believing that He will do as He has promised: "Yet to all who received him, to those who believed

in his name, he gave the right to become children of God" (John 1:12). "Here I am! I stand at the door and knock. If anyone hears my voice and opens the door, I will go in and eat with him, and he with me" (Revelation 3:20).

"But I have received Him many times, and nothing has happened," you say. Think that through. Did you really mean business? Did you surrender your will to Him? If so, then is God lying to you, failing to keep His part of the bargain? Impossible! The problem must be on your part. Maybe you are depending on feelings instead of upon what God has said in His Word.

What did He say? "Here I am! I stand at the door and knock. If anyone hears my voice and opens the door, I will go in and eat with him, and he with me."

If you opened the door of your life to Christ, then believe that He came in as He promised, no matter what your feelings may be. If you are not sure that you have received Him, stop and do so right now. Confess your sins to Him and ask Him to come into your life. Write down in your Bible, "I (your name) received Jesus Christ as my Savior and Lord on (date). Then when Satan tries to make you doubt, you can show him what you have written. More than that, you can show him what God promises in His word to those who receive Him, verses like Revelation 3:20 and John 1:12. He cannot stand before that authority.

When we receive Christ we are born into God's family. At first we are spiritual babies, whether we are six or sixty. Babies are not aware of many things, but as they grow they become more and more aware. As you read the Bible, talk to God, and fellowship with other Christians, you will grow spiritually. That inner assurance that you are God's child and without a doubt are bound for heaven *will come.*

It was because I had this assurance that I did not give up in complete despair in my dark tunnel. God brought me *through,* and He will do the same for you. But first, you must let Him come into your life.

24

Do I Want Deliverance?

"Do you want to get well?"

I was startled by the words in Hannah Whitall Smith's book *The Christian's Secret of a Happy Life*. Of course I wanted to be delivered from my depression, to live a happy, normal life again. Had I not quit taking my tranquilizers several months before in an effort to be as normal as possible? Had I not been trying in many other ways to conquer my depression by getting back to my writing, albeit half-heartedly, fixing up the house a little, having friends in occasionally, making myself try new recipes— even if these activities brought only momentary relief? Of course I wanted to be well.

Or did I?

Jesus asked the crippled man at the Pool of Bethesda, "Do you want to get well?" (John 5:6). Now He was asking me.

I searched my heart. Were there advantages in being unwell that I was reluctant to give up? Yes, there were advantages. For one thing, I was free from all responsibility outside of my home. Nobody expected me to teach a Sunday school class, to visit the sick, or to entertain as I had done before. I could skip church if I felt like it without being criticized. I "wasn't well."

Then, too, my husband was giving me more attention than I had ever had from him in my life. Although a busy pastor with many people to attend to, he would always take time out to counsel and pray with me when I had one of my crying jags. No matter how difficult and unreasonable I became, he was simply too chivalrous to fight with me. After all, I was sick! My three teenage sons were also extra considerate, thinking of little ways to cheer me and make me happy. The friends at church were extremely kind. In some ways, I had it made.

Did I want to give up all this extra attention and understanding and face the grim realities of life again? Did I want to give up my sessions of self-pity and go back to shouldering the responsibilities of a pastor's wife?

I thought it through, and when Jesus asked me again, "Do you want to get well?" I answered, "Yes." If I had answered in the negative or simply ignored the question, I believe I would still be in the tunnel.

Obviously there are kinds of depression other than the kind I experienced and about which I have written in this book. I cannot prescribe a cure for the other types with which I am not familiar. All I can do is tell you how I was delivered and recommend the same path for you if you are going through a tunnel similar to mine.

"God helps those who help themselves" is not in the Bible, although many people think it is. There is an element of truth in this statement, but I do not agree completely with it; besides, when you are in a tunnel as I was, you cannot help yourself. God is the One who can help us in a situation like this, but even God cannot help us if we will not let Him. "All the king's horses and all the king's men couldn't put Humpty Dumpty back together again." All the psychiatrists, counselors, books, even God Himself, cannot put *you* back together again unless you *want* to be made a whole person.

God will not pull you out of your tunnel against your will. He never violates an individual's free will. But if we are willing to come out of our darkness into the light, He will show us the way. I know, because He showed me.

First you must be *willing* to give up your depression.

"Willing!" you exclaim. "Of course I am willing! I'd do anything to get rid of it."

Are you sure? Giving up your depression also means giving up self-pity. Are you willing to part with this companion? She is miserable company, but there is something attractive about her, and we are loath to let her go. If we part with her, we must also give up her twin sister, grumbling.

Are you willing to change your pattern of thinking? Paul said, "Your attitude should be the same as that of Christ Jesus" (Philippians 2:5). God is ready to help you with your thought life, but you must cooperate with Him. You must obey His command to deliberately fix your mind on what is lovely, pure, and good instead of on negative, discouraging things.

Are you willing to replace worry with trust, turn all your cares over to Him and leave them there? Are you willing to build trust thoughts into your life by reading God's Word, committing it to memory, and meditating upon it? Are you willing to feed your mind only upon that which will inform, instruct, and inspire? Are you willing to believe God's promises instead of Satan's lies?

Are you willing to see God in everything? Will you believe in His love for you no matter what happens? Praise Him no matter what happens? Will you begin your day with thanks to Him and continue thanking Him all day long?

Will you accept yourself as God has made you? Will you accept the other people God has put into your life, recognizing that He is using them to perfect you? Will you accept the circumstances of your life, firmly believing that all things work together for good to them that love God?

Will you accept His forgiveness, His cleansing from sin, His peace? Will you base your happiness on nothing else but your hope in Christ?

Whether you are an occasional tunnel dweller or a permanent resident, if you are willing to put into practice these principles, you will be delivered. God says through Isaiah, "If you are willing and obedient, you will eat the best from the land" (Isaiah 1:19).

And how good it is! I have found it to be so. That is why I wrote this book. I felt I must share with my tunnel-mates the way out—into the light. It is so great out here; the air is so fresh and invigorating. There is peace and purpose. There is so much to do. Everything makes sense. Come, join me out in the sunshine.

Jesus asks you as He asked me, "Do you want to get well?" I hope you will answer yes, because as much as He wants to, He cannot help you unless you are willing.

25

If Your Loved One Is in a Tunnel

I was very fortunate during my days of depression to have an understanding husband and children. Others I have heard of are not so fortunate. The relative of a friend of mine was suffering from depression. She longed for the sympathy and understanding of her family, but she did not get it. She felt so totally misunderstood and unloved that in desperation she committed suicide.

It is not easy to live with a depressed person. Often they are not only gloomy but also unreasonable. Sometimes you feel like spanking them, other times like ignoring them completely in their misery and self-pity. But do not do either; they need your help so desperately. Be patient, kind, and loving—especially, be loving. When a person knows he is loved, everything is easier to face.

Perhaps your loved one needs professional counsel from a psychiatrist, psychologist, or clergyman. Try to find a counselor who has a personal relationship with Christ. Then he can help your loved one spiritually as well as psychologically. My psychiatrist was admittedly not a born-again man, so could not understand my Christian position. Soon after I was released from the hospital I stopped going to him. My pastor-husband became my psychiatrist, spending many hours counseling me. He was able to tie spiritual principles in with the psychological and therefore help the "whole me." Since much mental depression springs from spiritual causes, it is important to be counseled by a spiritual person, one who knows God and the principles of His Word as well as understanding psychology.

Maybe the depressed person in your family has already had professional counseling and still suffers. You can do much to help by patiently listening to his problems, pointing him to Jesus Christ, and reminding him of God's great plan for him. You can encourage him to practice the principles set forth in this book: to see God in everything and to give thanks for everything.

There are two harmful extremes in dealing with a depressed person. One is to tell him to quit acting like a baby and snap out of it. This treatment will only plunge him more deeply into despair. The other extreme is to be overly sympathetic. This, too, is a mistake, since it will make the depressed person feel even more sorry for himself than he already does. Recognize that he has a very real problem, but show him that it is not a hopeless one. There is a way out. Try to lead him step by step out of his misery, all the while endeavoring to maintain a cheerful, optimistic attitude yourself.

My husband always encouraged me by his reassurance that I was getting better. Even now, when I become overwhelmed occasionally, he encourages me by pointing out a reason for my distress. "You have had a lot of company," he reminds me, "and have been too busy in the church. Anyone would buckle under such a strain. But with a little rest you'll be yourself again." And I always am. But making me feel like a normal person who has a reason for being overwhelmed, instead of like a hopeless neurotic, gives me courage, hope, and optimism. Psychiatrists tell us that the most important thing they can give their patients is hope. Don't fail to impart this precious commodity to your depressed loved one.

Someday your patience, love, and encouragement will pay off. Your loved one will be out of the tunnel. God will use *you* to help him find happiness and meaning in life again. Do not give up. He needs you so much!

26

Rejoice!

Talking to a neighbor one day, I was telling her how good it is to know Christ and be assured of heaven. She replied, "It's not heaven I'm interested in so much. The thing that attracts me is that the Christians I know seem so happy and confident."

After my neighbor left I thought about what she had said. I wondered how many times I had turned people away from Christ by *not* being happy and confident. I began to realize that making Christians depressed is one of Satan's most effective tricks. He probably does not mind too much if we go to church regularly, read the Bible faithfully, work hard in the Lord's service, or even pray, as long as we remain gloomy and negative. Because a gloomy, negative Christian will not attract anybody to Christ.

Our enemy works overtime these days because he knows his time is short. We can hardly believe the accounts that we hear about satanic churches and devil worshipers. Equally disturbing are the reports of apostasy in many denominations, the immorality that has become a way of life for many, the lawlessness that sweeps our land, the corruption in government, the pollution contaminating our cities.

Of course these things sadden us, but we need to remember that for the Christian they are but signs that our Lord's coming is near. Jesus said, "When these things begin to take place, stand up and lift up your heads, because your redemption is drawing near" (Luke 21:28). Throw back your shoulders and rejoice, Christian. Something wonderful is about to happen!

Why should we be discouraged and worried? These evil conditions are not going to last forever. Jesus is coming to take us to be with Himself one of these days. As a child I remember the old-time Christians testifying about "going to glory." We do not use that word for heaven very much anymore, but it is a fitting description. Peter says we are called "to his eternal glory" (1 Peter 5:10). The Christian has a glorious future; we should rejoice instead of becoming gloomy. We have light and hope in a dark and hopeless world and glory just around the corner.

Philippians is the epistle of rejoicing; yet Paul wrote it while in prison. If he could rejoice in prison, can we not rejoice in the circumstances in which we find ourselves, whatever they may be? The Bible does not tell us to rejoice if we feel like it or to praise God when we're in the mood. Over and over again we are commanded to rejoice in the Lord, to praise God at all times, to offer Him the sacrifice of true thanks no matter what happens, whether we feel like it or not. It takes effort to rejoice, but once we begin, it is no longer difficult. We soon *feel* like rejoicing. We *feel* happy.

There is a time for sorrow, when we have sinned.
We are right to sorrow over wrong attitudes and
actions. "Godly sorrow brings repentance" (2 Corinthians 7:10). How often we need to cry with the
psalmist, "Create in me a pure heart, O God, and
renew a steadfast spirit within me" (Psalm 51:10).
God wants us to repent of our sins, but He does not
want us to continue to mourn over them after we
have been forgiven. This is unbelief. This grieves
Him.

When the people of Ezra's day heard the Word of
God read and explained, they saw their sin and
became extremely sorrowful. They wept as they realized how disobedient they had been. God saw
their sorrow for sin and their repentance. Graciously
He forgave them. Then He said to them through
Ezra, " 'Do not mourn or weep. . . . Do not grieve,
for the joy of the Lord is your strength' " (Nehemiah
8:9-10). In other words, He was saying, "I have forgiven you. Be happy. Rejoice. Even as you do this
you will find strength against further sin and failure."

God says the same to us today. Wipe away your
tears, Christian. Are you anxious, dejected, complaining, and sad? You do not need to stay that way.
You can ask God right now to forgive you for your
discouragement, for listening to Satan who tells you
to feel sorry for yourself. You can start right now
counting your blessings and praising God. As you
praise God, He will fill you with His joy. It will be
contagious; Christians with whom you associate
will be uplifted, and non-Christians will be attract-
ed to Christ.

Isaiah speaks of "beauty instead of ashes, the oil

of gladness instead of mourning, and a garment of praise instead of a spirit of despair" (Isaiah 61:3). God has provided this for us. All we have to do is take it by faith. Do you want beauty and joy instead of ashes, mourning, and heaviness? *Put on the garment of praise!* And keep it on *all day long!* If you are not wearing the garment of praise, you are not properly dressed!

"Praise the Lord. How good it is to sing praises to our God, how pleasant and fitting to praise him!" (Psalm 147:1). "Let us come before him with thanksgiving" (Psalm 95:2).

"I will sing to the Lord all my life; I will sing praise to my God as long as I live. . . . I rejoice in the Lord" (Psalm 104:33-34).

"Now may the Lord of peace himself give you peace at all times and in every way" (2 Thessalonians 3:16).

"Finally . . . rejoice in the Lord! (Philippians 3:1); "for the joy of the Lord is your strength" (Nehemiah 8:10).